# WEAPON

# THE ROCKET PROPELLED GRENADE

## GORDON L. ROTTMAN

Series Editor Martin Pegler

First published in Great Britain in 2010 by Osprey Publishing, Midland House, West Way, Botley, Oxford, OX2 0PH, UK
44-02 23rd Street, Suite 219, Long Island City, NY 11101, USA

E-mail: info@ospreypublishing.com

A CIP catalog record for this book is available from the British Library

Print ISBN: 978 1 84908 153 5

PDF e-book ISBN: 978 1 84908 154 2

Page layout by Ben Salvesen

Index by Fineline Editorial Services

Typeset in Sabon and Univers

Originated by PDQ Media

Printed in China through Worldprint

10 11 12 13 14    10 9 8 7 6 5 4 3 2 1

## Editor's note

The following data will help in comparing the imperial and metric measurements:

1 mile = 1.6km
1 yard = 0.9m
1ft = 0.3m
1in. = 2.54cm/25.4mm
1 ton (US) = 0.9 tonnes
1lb = 0.45kg
1 gal = 4.5 liters

## Artist's note

Readers may care to note that the original paintings from which the color battlescenes in this book were prepared were available for private sale. All reproduction copyright whatsoever is retained by the Publishers. All inquiries should be addressed to:

Ramiro Bujeiro, C.C. 28, 1602 Florida, Argentina

The Publishers regret that they can enter into no correspondence upon this matter.

## Acknowledgements

The author is deeply indebted to Beryl Barnett for the loan of manuals, books, materials, and the opportunity to photograph his collection of communist bloc ordnance. Much thanks goes to William L. Howard of the Ordnance Technical Intelligence Museum, Largo, Florida for his valuable help in providing research materials and encouragement. Joseph S. Bermudez, Jr kindly provided scarce information on North Korean RPGs. The author much appreciates the information and insight on RPGs provided by Edward Rudnicki of Picatinny Arsenal, the Russian translation provided by Berry Rhoades, information on the US-made RPG-7 provided by Jim Cihak of Airtronic USA, and translation advice provided by Burkhard Schulze. The 705th Ordnance Company (Explosive Ordnance Disposal), Fort Polk, Louisiana provided valuable background materials for which the author is grateful. A special thanks goes to various manufacturers and exporters for their assistance:

Airtronic USA, Inc., Elk Grove Village, Illinois
Bydgoskie Zaklady Electromechanical Works BELMA SA, Lochowska, Poland
Cenzin Company Limited Foreign Trade Enterprise, Warsaw, Poland
Konstrukta Defence, Trencín, Slovakia
North China Industries Corporation, Beijing, China
Saab Training Systems, Huskvarna, Sweden
Talley Defense Systems, Mesa, Arizona

## Abbreviations

| | |
|---|---|
| AFV | armored fighting vehicle |
| APC | armored personnel carrier |
| AT | antitank |
| ATGM | antitank guided missile |
| ERA | explosive reactive armor |
| FAM | fuel-air munition |
| HE | high-explosive |
| HEAT | high-explosive antitank (shaped-charge warhead) |
| HE/frag | high-explosive/fragmentation |
| LAW | Light Antitank Weapon |
| MILES | Multiple Integrated Laser Engagment System |
| NVA | North Vietnamese Army |
| PG | *Protivotankovii Granata* (antitank grenade) |
| RPG | *Ruchnoi Protivotankovii Granatomet* (hand antitank grenade launcher) |
| US | United States |
| USSR | Union of Soviet Socialist Republics |
| VC | Viet Cong |

Front cover: An RPG-7-armed Lebanese soldier stands guard at a checkpoint. (© Ed Kashi/Corbis)

# CONTENTS

# INTRODUCTION

The RPG-series of antitank projectors are perhaps the most widely used shoulder-fired antitank weapons in the world today. Used by scores of armies, militias, insurgents and terrorists, RPGs have been used not only against their intended targets – armored fighting vehicles (AFVs) – but against personnel, fortifications, buildings, soft-skin vehicles, watercraft, and aircraft. Lightweight, relatively compact, easy to conceal, comparatively inexpensive, easy to operate and maintain, they meet most of the requirements of any armed group. In addition to all this they are reliable, effective, and lethal. Like any weapon system, of course, RPGs and their ammunition have their limitations. But while proponents of more advanced weapons such as wire-guided or laser-guided missiles frequently tout these limitations, they lose sight of many armed groups' requirements for weapons that are lightweight, compact, inexpensive, and easy to operate and maintain. Most sophisticated systems tend to be the exact opposite, and – owing to export controls and restrictions – are also more difficult to obtain. To be effective, an army needs a mix of both sophisticated and uncomplicated weapons. Although the limitations of the RPG and its terminal target effects are often cited, this author, having been on the receiving end of RPG-2 and 7 fires, can attest to their effectiveness.

There are several models of RPG, such as the reloadable RPG-2, 7, 16, 29, and 32,[1] along with the single-shot, throwaway RPG-18, 22, 26, 27, and 30. There are also similar single-shot weapons made by Eastern European countries designated "RPG": the Czechoslovak RPG-75 (*Reaktivni Protitankova* or *Pancéřovka*) and Polish RPG-76 (*Rêczny Ppanc Granatnik*).

[1] The 105mm RPG-29 *Vampir* (Vampire) of 1989 is a very different weapon from earlier RPGs; it is more similar to the US Marine Corps' 83mm Mk 153 Mod 1 Shoulder-launched Multipurpose Assault Weapon (SMAW). The 105mm RPG-32 *Hashim* was produced in 2007 for use by Jordan; it is a small reloadable weapon with the rocket in a modular tube. These weapons are breech-loaded and outside the scope of this book.

**OPPOSITE**

An Afghanistan National Army soldier carries an RPG-7 and two additional rounds, which have been tied together for easy handling. (© Ed Darack/Science Faction/Corbis)

"RPG" is normally translated into English as "rocket propelled grenade," but in fact it means *Reaktivnoi Protivotankovii Granatomet* (hand antitank grenade launcher). Most models can best be technically described not as "rocket propelled grenades" but as recoilless antitank projectors. RPG can also mean *Reaktivnoi Protivotankovii Granati* (antitank rocket grenade). This latter term refers to the single-shot, disposable models. Slight differences in the spelling of these terms will be found when transliterated from Cyrillic. The term "antitank grenade" (*Protivotankovii Granati* – or PG) is used to identify high-explosive antitank (HEAT) projectiles, while in East Germany the "PG" was translated as *Panzergranate* ([anti]armor grenade).

First test-fielded in 1954, the RPG-2 was a "recoilless weapon" and *not* a "rocket launcher"; the projectile was launched by a propellant cartridge similar to that used by the non-reloadable German *Panzerfaust* first used during World War II. In contrast, the RPG-7 and 16 are "rocket-assisted recoilless weapons"; a propellant cartridge launches the projectile and a rocket booster ignites almost immediately after launching to increase the projectile's velocity and range. The single-shot, disposable RPG-18, 22, 26, 27, and 30 variants are true "rocket launchers." Therefore, technically the term "rocket launcher" does not apply to most Soviet/Russian RPGs and German *Panzerfaust* weapons even though the term is widely used to describe them. The term "RPG" also refers to three antitank hand grenades, the RPG-40, 43, and 6 (1944), which were fielded by the Soviets during World War II and remained in postwar use. In this instance "RPG" simply means *Ruchnoi Protivotankovii Granati* (hand antitank grenade).

World War II witnessed the first explosion in antitank technology, with developments including rifles, grenades, and even recoilless weapons such as the *Panzerfaust*. However, it was the use of the RPG-7 during the Vietnam War which heralded a new era in antitank weaponry. Moreover, the RPG-series of weapons rapidly developed unforeseen uses, including as antiaircraft and antipersonnel weapons, all frequently in the hands of combatants with minimal training or experience. No wonder then that the RPG is widely considered one of the most revolutionary weapons ever to have been created, and one that is destined to dominate the battlefield for years to come.

# DEVELOPMENT
## Six decades of antitank technology

### ANTITANK WEAPONS IN WORLD WAR II

The widespread employment of tanks in World War II caused armies to react with major changes in infantry organization, tactics, and armament. The USSR, like most of the belligerent nations, entered the war with basically four types of infantry antitank weapons: light antitank guns, antitank rifles, antitank rifle grenades, and antitank hand grenades and hand-delivered charges.

### Antitank guns

Antitank guns found at battalion and regimental levels were typically in the 37mm-caliber range, although the Soviets used both 37mm and 45mm guns. These were relatively large, heavy weapons mounted on two-wheel carriages and towed by light vehicles. They could be manhandled short distances over rough terrain, but they were difficult to conceal and time-consuming to dig in. They were also difficult to relocate quickly to a new position, which was essential for survival. By 1941 these guns were obsolete as antitank weapons owing to improvements in armor and tank design. They remained in employment only because larger-caliber replacements were slow to become available, and because they had their uses against other targets.

### Antitank rifles

Antitank rifles were usually provided on the basis of one per platoon. These weapons were a challenge to carry, being heavier and bulkier than machine guns, and did little damage to a tank even if they managed to penetrate the armor. The Germans and Poles issued 7.9mm rifles, the British

One of the most used Soviet antitank weapons during World War II was the massive 14.5mm PTRD-41 antitank rifle. It was heavy, cumbersome, and not very effective as a tank-killer. (Nik Cornish/STAVKA)

the .55in (13.97mm) Boys rifle – nicknamed variously "the elephant gun," or "Charlie the Bastard" according to nationality – and the Soviets a 14.5mm (.56cal) monster. Antitank rifles were obsolete by 1940 but some soldiered on; the Soviets, the most prevalent user, retained them throughout the Great Patriotic War of 1941–45.

## Antitank rifle grenades

Antitank rifle grenades made their debut in 1940, and were used first by the Germans and British, followed by the Americans and Soviets. They represented the first use of the "shaped-charge" warhead, newly perfected by all of these armies. Initially rifle grenade launchers were issued on the basis of one per squad, but they proved to be of only marginal effectiveness as an antitank weapon. While they were certainly light enough, their accurate range was less than 100m and their armor penetration and effects on a tank were limited. The size of their warheads was limited by the fact that if they were too heavy they would cause excessive recoil. Although they remained in use and were improved in most armies, the Soviets withdrew their dismal VPGS-41 in 1943 to rely on their antitank rifles.

## Antitank hand grenades and hand-delivered antitank charges

Antitank hand grenades were essentially last-resort weapons and almost certain to guarantee infantrymen an award for valor, usually posthumously. Their throwing range was less than 20m, with limited penetration and effects. Larger hand-delivered antitank charges were even more dangerous, as the attacker had to physically attach them to the tank by magnets or adhesive. This allowed them to contain heavier bursting charges, but for the attacker this often ensured it was a one-way trip. Most relied on shaped-charges, but some early devices were simply heavy bursting charges to shatter or spall the armor plate.[1]

What was needed was an antitank weapon light and compact enough for an infantryman to carry on the battlefield, allowing him to keep pace with the rest of his platoon. The weapon needed to be both reliable and

[1] Spalling is the effect of a heavy explosive charge detonating against the outside of armor and "budging" it inward to cause fragments to burst off the inside surface at high speed and in effect become shrapnel.

simple to operate, requiring minimal training. The factor of overriding importance was the weapon's ability to defeat the enemy's main battle tanks – if not with a frontal hit, then at least with a side shot. That was a great deal to expect of a small, light handheld weapon.

## The shaped-charge

The shaped-charge (or hollow-charge) high-explosive antitank (HEAT) warhead was perfected on the eve of World War II. This revolutionary weapon came to be widely used in hand and rifle grenades, antitank and tank guns, antitank rocket launchers, recoilless guns, field artillery, and hand-emplaced demolition charges. Shaped-charge munitions rely on a principle known as the "Munroe effect," named after its American inventor, Charles E. Munroe, a 19th-century professor at the US Naval Academy. He did not perfect it as an armor-penetrating charge; he simply demonstrated its potential effect in 1888 in experiments using static charges against steel plates.

The principle employs an explosive charge with a cone-shaped cavity. The cavity is placed against the target, and focuses the blast on a small point and cuts a hole through it. Early shaped-charges had a comparatively shallow cavity. During World War I a German, Egon Neumann, improved the concept by lining the cavity with thin metal and detonating the charge not directly against the metal surface but a short distance from it to further focus the blast, a distance two to three times the diameter of the charge. In 1935–38, a Swiss engineer, Henri J. Mohaupt, perfected the principle and demonstrated its use. In October 1941 he came to the US and worked on the bazooka (antitank rocket launcher) project. An unnamed British engineer observing the demonstrations surmised the concept, and designed

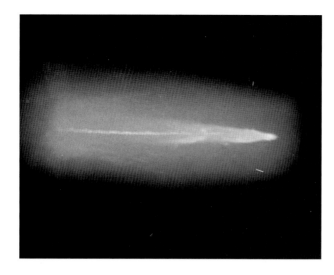

the first shaped-charge rifle grenade. It was Germany, however, which first used the shaped-charge in combat (as the *Hohlladung* or hollow-charge) when on May 11, 1940, glider-landed German paratroopers used hollow-charges to destroy gun turrets in the formidable Belgium fortress of Eben Emael.

One of the main benefits of shaped-charge projectiles is that they do not rely on velocity or mass to penetrate armor. A shaped-charge round will achieve the same penetration at 500m range as it will at 50m. It makes no difference if the projectile is hand-thrown or fired from a high-velocity gun. While such different types of projectiles must by necessity be of different designs, if they could theoretically be of the same size and design the penetration would be exactly the same.

The projectile is comparatively light and inexpensive as no hardened steel penetrator or extensive casting or machining is required. Armor two to three times the diameter of the cone can be penetrated. Upon impact the projectile is detonated by a base-detonating fuze, and the metal lining is transformed into two separate components of the blast. Part of the liner vaporizes and punches through the armor plate at approximately 10,000m/s – 30 times the speed of sound. Formed as the base of the jet is a molten "hot solid slug." Its tip moves faster than the base, causing it to "stretch" as it travels. This slug does not contribute to the penetration effect and may not even enter the hole caused by the explosive jet. However, if the slug follows the jet through the hole it will inflict ballistic damage inside the target. The process is usually described as the liner being "vaporized into a plasma jet that instantly burns through armor." This is not entirely correct. This jet carries with it fragments

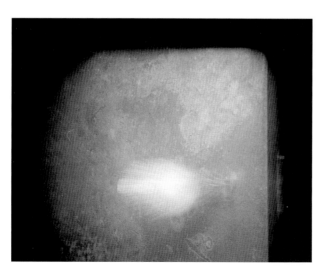

from both the projectile and the armor, and the penetration itself is a kinetic process; it doesn't burn through. The jet and fragments ignite ammunition and fuel and kill anyone in their path. The initial entry hole is surprisingly small in diameter, just millimeters across. But the outer entry hole is still larger in diameter than the interior exit hole. In addition to penetrating armor, shaped-charges will penetrate concrete, masonry, timber, and sandbags.

Fin-stabilized shaped-charges have more effective penetration than spin-stabilized projectiles, as they either do not rotate or do so at a very slow rate. The high rate of spin imparted on spin-stabilized projectiles dissipates up to three-quarters of the penetrating effect through centrifugal force. This results in a broader and shallower penetrating effect.

The explosive filler in PG-2 HEAT rounds is 50 percent TNT and 50 percent RDX. RDX (Research Department Explosive), perfected by the British late in World War II, is one of the more powerful explosives with more brisance (shattering effect) than TNT, making it ideal for shaped-charges. It is also highly stable and stores well. RDX is white in color and detonates with a white or light-gray smoke. PG-7 and PG-7M warheads developed for use in the RPG-7 are filled with 94 percent RDX and 6 percent wax – called A-IX-1 or *geksogen* (hexogen) by the Soviets. The more modern warheads are filled with 96 percent HMX and 4 percent wax, with the Russian designation of OKFOL/OL.

## ORIGINS OF THE RPG-SERIES

It is surprising that the Soviets failed to field a practical antitank rocket launcher during the Great Patriotic War as they had such a desperate need for one. They were familiar with the US 2.36in (60mm) M1 antitank rocket launcher, or bazooka (having been provided with 8,500 of these in late 1942[2]) as well as with the *Panzerfaust* from 1943, and they had their own well-developed *Katyusha* rocket program. Instead the Soviets persisted with their antitank rifle and grenades, and used all the *Panzerfäuste* they could lay their hands on, along with German magnetic hand-mines.

The Soviets had attempted to field an antitank rocket launcher, the RS-65, in 1931. This was a very crude and heavy 65mm shoulder-fired weapon. Its warhead relied on blast effect as the shaped-charge had not yet been perfected. The cumbersome weapon was none too effective and was dropped. The next attempt was the 82mm SPG-82 rocket launcher (*Stankovii Protivotankovii Granatomet* – mounted antitank grenade launcher). Its development began in 1942 and it saw limited fielding in 1944. This weapon was distinctly Soviet in its design – crude and unrefined. It was unnecessarily heavy at 38kg, overly long at 2,100mm, fitted with a large, awkward shield, and mounted on a two-wheel carriage which was

When a shaped-charge projectile detonates against armor plate, the cone's liner collapses into two distinct parts. The jet is the long cylindrical rod of liner metal that does the actual penetrating. It is distinguished by having a velocity gradient throughout its length, with the tip moving faster than the base – which is what causes jet breakup and decline in penetration at excessive standoff distances. The slug is formed at the base of the jet and contributes nothing to penetration, and may not even pass through the hole formed by the jet. This series of high-speed photographs of a shaped-charge detonation and impact is from a US Army test of *c.* 1950. (Time & Life Pictures/Getty Images)

[2] It was these captured *Lend-Liza* bazookas that spawned the development of the 8.8cm *Panzerschreck*, not bazookas captured from the US in Tunisia as is commonly assumed. Bazookas captured in Tunisia were, however, tested by the Germans.

A German ordnance sergeant demonstrates the *Panzerfaust 60* to officers. The *Panzerfaust* was not reloadable. The 140mm warhead could be removed, but the pre-loaded propellant change was retained in the launcher tube. (Nik Cornish/STAVKA)

too low to the ground. This heavy, oversized weapon was the opposite of the concept of an easily portable antitank weapon, as the bazooka and *Panzerfaust* were. Its HEAT round was also made less effective because of a point-detonating fuze. These ungainly characteristics, coupled with its mere 300m practical range and 175mm armor penetration – little better than the far lighter and more wieldy bazooka – immediately sent the Red Army in search of an alternative tank-killer.

The American M1 antitank rocket launcher or "bazooka" was fielded in late 1942 and proved to be highly effective. It became even more so with the development of the M1A1, M9, and M9A1. Depending on the model it weighed 5.85kg or 7.2kg, had a 230–275m range, and could penetrate up to 110mm of armor. The British took a different route with their Mk I Projector, Infantry, Anti-Tank or PIAT (pronounced "pee-at"). This was a very different weapon to the *Panzerfaust* and bazooka, weighing almost as much as the .55in Boys antitank rifle it replaced. Although rocket-boosted, it revealed no telltale back blast like other rocket weapons.

Besides the bazooka, it was the *Panzerfaust* that had the most influence on the RPG-series. Several models of the *Panzerfaust* were developed and fielded between 1943 and 1945: *Panzerfaust 30 klein* (small) and *30 gross* (large) both in October 1943; *60* in September 1944; *100* in November 1944; and *150* in January 1945, with the *60* and *100* the most widely used. The designations refer to the weapons' approximate effective range. The earlier models had large-caliber, hemispherical warheads. The warhead could be removed, but the propellant charge remained in the tube. In an effort to provide a more effective and accurate weapon, the *Panzerfaust 150* was developed with a smaller-diameter, more streamlined warhead, but still

## The *Panzerfaust*

For comparison with RPGs, the characteristics of various models of *Panzerfaust* are provided here.

|  | *Pzf.30 gross* | *Pzf.60* | *Pzf.100* | *Pzf.150* |
|---|---|---|---|---|
| Launcher caliber | 44mm (1.73in) | 50mm (1.97in) | 60mm (2.36in) | 60mm (2.36in) |
| Warhead caliber | 140mm (5.5in) | 140mm (5.5in) | 140mm (5.5in) | 105mm (4.13in) |
| Length with warhead | 1,045mm (41.1in) | 1,045mm (41.1in) | 1,045mm (41.1in) | 1,051mm (41.3in) |
| Loaded weight | 5.1kg (11.23lb) | 6.1kg (13.4lb) | 6.8kg (15lb) | 6kg+ (13lb+) |
| Muzzle velocity | 30m/s (98fps) | 45m/s (148fps) | 62m/s (203fps) | 82m/s (269fps) |
| Effective range | 30m (100ft) | 60m (200ft) | 100m (330ft) | 150m (490ft) |
| Armor penetration | 200mm (7.8in) for all models | | | |

over-caliber. While improvements over earlier models included a pistol grip and normal trigger, the *150* was still a single-shot, throwaway weapon. The *Panzerfaust 150* saw only very limited use in the war's final months.

Another *Panzerfaust* was under development at the war's end and featured a major departure from earlier versions. Besides having a much longer effective range, it was also reloadable. This was the *Panzerfaust 250*, and both the Americans and Soviets captured plans for this weapon. Although the American Ordnance Department studied it at Aberdeen Proving Ground, no need was seen for a similar weapon as the US already possessed the 2.36in (60mm) bazooka, and a much-improved 3.5in (89mm) model had been standardized in late 1945. On the other hand the Soviets, lacking a comparable weapon, adopted many aspects of the *Panzerfaust 250*'s design and developed a new weapon, the RPG-1.

Like the *Panzerfaust 150* the *250* had a pistol grip, normal trigger, and percussion firing system (ignition cartridge and firing pin). Prior to the *150*, all models had a lever-type trigger atop the launcher tube that fired an ignition cartridge contained within the projectile's stabilizer tube. The *Panzerfaust 250* also used the *150*'s streamlined warhead, but with an igniter primer fitted in the tailboom that aligned with the percussion firing pin contained in the pistol grip's firing mechanism. The idea behind the *250* was that providing a reloadable weapon would require fewer material resources than having to furnish every warhead with a firing system, sights, and launcher tube. It would also require less shipping space and fewer packaging materials. However, the trade-off was that the individual weapon was heavier and required a two-man crew.

The Germans developed another antitank rocket weapon in 1943, the 88mm *Raketenpanzerbüchse R.Pz.B.43*, which was based on the bazooka and even known to the German soldier by the same nickname, *Ofenrohr* ("stovepipe"), as well as being called the *Panzerschreck* ("armor-terror"). Improved versions, the *R.Pz.B.54* and *54/1*, appeared in 1944.

Germany sold allied Finland *Panzerfäuste*, which they called the *Panssarikauhu*. The *Panzerfaust* was held under the arm for firing, rather than on the shoulder like the bazooka and RPG. (Courtesy Concord Publications)

## The RPG–*Panzerfaust* connection

The origins of the RPG-2 are often said to lie in the *Panzerfaust*. However, while the weapons possess similarities, there are many significant differences. There are several claims regarding the Soviet use of the *Panzerfaust* and the RPG-1, the most popular of which are listed below:

- Soviets designated captured German *Panzerfäuste* the RPG-1.
- Soviets took over captured German factories and continued producing *Panzerfäuste* as the RPG-1.
- Soviets captured the plans and/or reverse-engineered the *Panzerfaust* and produced it in their own factories as the RPG-1.
- Soviets moved the manufacturing equipment to the USSR and produced their own version of the *Panzerfaust* as the RPG-1.

None of these are true. The Red Army did capture and use *Panzerfäuste*, which they nicknamed *Fausts*, as they had no comparable man-portable antitank weapons. So many *Fausts* were captured that the average rifleman became as familiar with them as with his own weapons. However, the Soviets did not produce their own *Panzerfäuste* from reverse-engineered examples as often claimed. They did not designate captured *Fausts* the "RPG-1" and nor did they manufacture *Panzerfäuste* for their own use in captured factories.

All *Panzerfaust* development and most production was carried out by Hugo Schneider A.G. (HASAG) in Leipzig-Schönefeld, 145km southwest of Berlin, and at a HASAG-operated plant at the Schlieben concentration camp 80km south of Berlin. Leipzig was occupied by US troops on April 20, 1945, 18 days before V-E Day, and the city was not turned over to the Soviets until July. The Schlieben plant was finally occupied by the Soviets on April 21. *Panzerfaust* production was carried out by slave labor at both Leipzig-Schönefeld and Schlieben. At Schlieben the Soviets found only 130 sick and weakened workers; some 5,000 had been evacuated just days before. Robert Tümmler Metallwarenfabrik in Döbeln, 145km south of Berlin, also produced *Panzerfäuste* and was the exclusive producer of the few *Panzerfaust 150s*. Unscathed Döbeln was occupied by Soviet troops on May 6, two days before V-E Day.

A German soldier fires a *Panzerfaust 60* demonstrating its considerable back blast and muzzle flash, throwing burning propellant particles forward. (TopFoto)

The Soviets could not possibly have put any of these factories into operation, especially since the delivery of raw materials and subcontracted components had already ceased. The launcher tubes, for example, had been fabricated by Volkswagen-Werke in Fallersleben; this had been occupied by US troops on April 18 and production had halted even earlier.

The *Panzerfaust* plants' machinery was not removed until some time after the war. The Soviets had already set about developing an improved weapon influenced by, but certainly not copied from, the *Panzerfaust* in 1944. The confiscated machinery may have been partly used or copied to produce the Soviets' own RPG-2, especially the projectiles, but not the RPG-1.

It is also said that these supposed Soviet RPG-1s were copies of the *Panzerfaust 100* or that the RPG-2 was literally copied from the *Panzerfaust*. However, the two weapons were of very different design, regardless of superficial similarities. The *Panzerfäuste* were single-shot throwaway weapons with crude sights and simplified percussion powder train firing mechanisms, without pistol grips. The RPG-1 and 2 were reloadable, and had improved sights, a rifle-like trigger and firing pin system, and a pistol grip.

One specific myth is that the RPG-2 was copied from the *Panzerfaust 150*. Although the *Panzerfaust 150*'s long, pointed warhead provided the basis for the RPG-2's PG-2 HEAT round, the rounds were in fact very different. The earlier *Panzerfäuste 30*, *60*, and *100* had proportionally larger, blunt-nosed warheads. Development of the Soviet RPG-1 had begun before the *100* was fielded in November 1944 and long before the factories were captured. A major difference between the RPG and the *Panzerschreck* and bazooka was that these latter weapons used an electrical system (magneto or batteries) to ignite the propellant. RPGs used percussion firing systems, that is, a trigger-released hammer striking a firing pin that strikes an ignition primer.

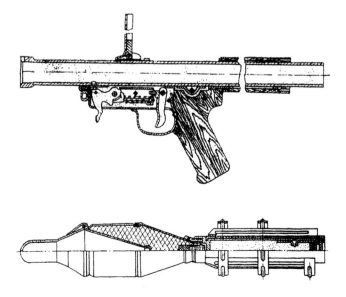

The uncocked firing mechanism of the RPG-1 (top) and a cutaway of the 70mm PG-1 HEAT projectile (bottom). The 30mm propellant cartridge is permanently fixed to the projectile and contained within the over-barrel outer sleeve and the three ring-type fins.

The RPG-2's grandfather was actually the *Panzerfaust 250*. This weapon was to be reloadable and had other features similar to the future RPG-2 including a trigger grip and an electrical firing system. It had a long pointed-nosed projectile similar to that of the *Panzerfaust 150* and was intended to replace earlier *Panzerfäuste* and the *Panzerschreck*. It was scheduled for introduction in September 1945 but was not even built in prototype form. Both the US and the USSR obtained plans for the *Panzerfaust 250*, and they heavily influenced the design of the RPG-1. Only a few RPG-1 prototypes were produced and they were not copies of the *Panzerfaust 250* or any other *Panzerfaust*, but a very different weapon.

## A NEW GENERATION OF ANTITANK WEAPONS: THE RPG-1 AND RPG-2

### The RPG-1

Soviet study of the *Panzerfaust, Panzerschreck,* and bazooka led to research for a new weapon, which would combine the most desirable features of these launchers with a primary aim of keeping the new weapon compact and light, yet still lethal to modern tanks. Headed by G. P. Lominskiy, lead design engineer at the Main Artillery Directorate's Small Arms and Mortar Research Range, development of the LPG-44 and its PG-70 HEAT round began in 1944. Prototypes were built and successfully test-fired, with the result that it was redesignated the RPG-1 in 1945, with the projectile now called the PG-1. This was a simple reloadable, shoulder-fired launcher fitted with a pistol grip and trigger for percussion firing. It had a flip-up leaf sight and no forward sight. To aim it the appropriate range aperture in the leaf sight was aligned on the top edge of the warhead and with the target, as with the *Panzerfaust*. The 1m tube had a wooden sheath to protect the firer from heat. The 70mm warhead was fitted with a short 30mm propellant cartridge that slid into the muzzle. Over this was a sleeve that slid over the barrel with three ring-fins for stabilization. Preparations were being made to put the RPG-1 into series production, but too many unsolvable problems developed with the projectile, mainly with the base-detonating fuze and inconsistent propellant ignition at different temperatures. It had a low velocity, which affected its accuracy against moving targets, a flat trajectory for only 50m of its 75m range, and it could penetrate only 150mm of armor, less than the *Panzerfaust*. Work continued until 1948 when it was cancelled.

The 1944 experimental 30mm RPG-1 (aka LPG-44) with its single post sight raised (it folds rearward) and the hammer in the cocked position. It was cancelled in 1948 owing to ammunition problems and the advent of the more promising RPG-2, development of which had begun the year before. (Drawing by Tony Bryan)

# The RPG-2

In 1947 the Ministry of Agriculture's GSKB-30 Machine-Building Design Bureau began development of the DRG-40 antitank weapon and its PG-80 projectile. It may seem odd that this was undertaken under the auspices of the Ministry of Agriculture, but GSKB-30 had fallen under the People's Commissariat for Munition Industry and was transferred to farm equipment production after the war. Clearly, however, the Bureau was still making good use of its arms experts. While the new weapon was superficially similar in design to the RPG-1, there were numerous improvements, especially in the warhead and propellant, which led to the demise of its predecessor. After successful testing the weapon was designated the RPG-2 and the 80mm projectile the PG-2 in 1948.

The RPG-2 was more rugged than the RPG-1 and had both rear and front sights. The caliber was 40mm, allowing for a larger propellant charge, which was also much lengthened over that of the RPG-1. It also had a much simpler, lighter, lower-cost fin assembly with minimal drag, a problem encountered with the PG-1. The propellant charge was separate from the projectile and screwed on to the base of the tailboom. In fact the 80mm projectile was so improved that it had twice the range, over twice the muzzle velocity, and a flatter trajectory for twice the range, as well as achieving one-third more penetration.

East German troops prepare to fire an RPG-2 during a winter training exercise. The assistant gunner is ensuring he is clear of the back blast area, and he would warn the gunner if the launcher was angled to cause the back blast to be deflected off the position's rear wall. (Alamy)

## RPG-1 characteristics

| | | |
|---|---|---|
| Bore caliber | 30mm | 1.18in |
| Warhead caliber | 70mm | 2.76in |
| Launcher length | 1,000mm | 39.36in |
| Projectile length | 425mm | 16.73in |
| Launcher weight | 2kg | 4.4lb |
| Projectile weight | 1.6kg | 3.52lb |
| Muzzle velocity | 40m/s | 131fps |
| Effective range | 75m | 82 yards |
| Armor penetration | 150mm | 6in |
| Rate of fire | 4–6rpm | |

## RPG-2 characteristics

| | | |
|---|---|---|
| Bore caliber | 40mm | 1.57in |
| Warhead caliber | 80mm | 3.15in |
| Launcher length | 950mm | 37.40in |
| Projectile length* | 665mm | 26.18in |
| Launcher weight | 2.86kg | 6.31lb |
| Projectile weight* | 1.84kg | 4.06lb |
| Muzzle velocity | 84m/s | 275fps |
| Effective range | 150m | 164 yards |
| Armor penetration | 200mm | 7.8in |
| Rate of fire | 4–6rpm | |
| *with propellant charge attached | | |

The RPG-2 was about as simple an antiarmor weapon as could be developed. It consisted of a straight 40mm tube fitted with a single pistol grip housing the trigger, percussion firing pin, and a simple safety. The tube's central portion (approximately half the tube's overall length) was covered by a wooden or – less commonly – composite plastic sheath, which served to protect the firer's cheek both from the chill of the steel tube in severe cold and from the heat generated by repeated firing. A removable, perforated flange on the breech end helped reduce foreign matter from entering if it was dragged on the ground, but this was frequently removed. Very simple folding front and rear iron sights were provided. There was no optical sight available, and nor was there any means to attach a night vision sight without modification as on the RPG-2N. The weapon was extremely reliable as there were very few moving parts and it required a real effort to break it.

The PG-2 HEAT projectile. The inverted cone of the shaped-charge is seen behind the nosecone. The black powder-filled propellant cartridge is attached.

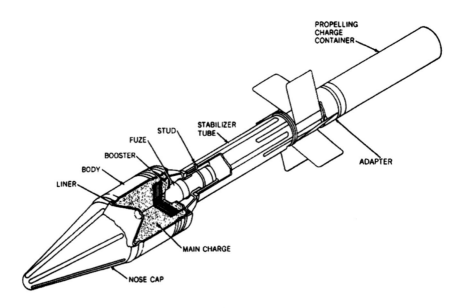

Nicaraguan/Cuban-backed rebels in El Salvador carry a Type 56 (Chinese-made RPG-2 copy), 1982. In Latin America RPGs are known as *bazukas*. After the 1980s the RPG-2 was little seen. Its ammunition production had ceased and remaining rounds were deteriorating. (TopFoto)

The PG-2 projectile is effective against stationary targets at 150m and moving targets at 100m. The maximum flight range is 600m without self-destruct and approximately 460m with the self-destruct capability fitted on later projectiles.

Light, compact, rugged, reliable, and simple to operate and maintain, the RPG-2, known as the *Granatomet*, was recognized as a very effective infantry light antitank weapon when it began to be fielded in 1954. Most first-line Soviet divisions received it within a year. Shortly afterward it was fielded by Warsaw Pact forces, and China adopted it in 1956 as the Type 56.

### Foreign-made versions of the RPG-2

The Chinese Type 56, the North Korean model of the RPG-2, and the North Vietnamese B40 were virtually identical to the Soviet-made RPG-2 except for markings and minor manufacturing details. (The "B" in B40 means "Ba do ka," Vietnamese for bazooka. The "40" represents its 40mm caliber.) The B40 designation was generally applied to all RPG-2s and Type 56s used by the North Vietnamese Army (NVA) and Viet Cong (VC) regardless of national origin. Neither the Type 56 nor the B40 were provided with the flange-like blast deflector. The rear portion of the B40's barrel guard was approximately 50mm shorter than those found on RPG-2s and Type 56s. Both Soviet and Chinese versions were used by the VC and the NVA. VC RPG-2s were occasionally found with a crude steel rod handgrip welded under the barrel midway between the trigger grip and muzzle to provide stability. When the 40mm RPG-7 was introduced it was simply designated the B41 to differentiate the two weapons. An example marking found on the trigger grip on a B40 is: CT2-S GIAI-PHONG (Liberate or Liberation, as in Giai Phong Mien Nam Viet Nam). The meaning of "CT2-S" is unknown. Others are marked B40 GIAI-PHONG.

The designation of the North Korean RPG-2 is unknown. There was a 1953 report of a "50mm Type 89 rocket launcher," but no details are available and no weapon matching this description has since come to light. The first mention of RPG-2s in North Korean service was in 1956; the weapons probably entered service in 1955. It is believed that these were Soviet-supplied and that North Korean production did not begin until after 1958/59 when licensing agreements for a number of weapons were concluded with the USSR.

Although the RPG-2 was effective from the outset, it was felt that it could be made more so. A longer range, improved accuracy, and increased lethality against rapidly improving tanks were needed. However no upgrades were to be made on the RPG-2 other than the installation of an infrared (IR) night sight, which was fitted to some from 1957 so that they became the RPG-2N. The NSP-2 sight consisted of an active infrared spotlight with an IR viewer and a heavy man-packed battery connected to the IR sight by a cable. The NSP-2 weighed 6kg and had a range of 150–200m under ideal conditions.

However, because of its small size, simplicity, and lack of an optical sight, in the West it was discounted as little more than just a crude grenade launcher not much better than the old rifle grenades. That proved to be a mistake. It missed the Korean War, but saw combat in the early 1960s in Vietnam when the true worth of the RPG became clear – both as an antiarmor weapon and as a man-portable artillery substitute.

For many years after it began to be replaced on a wholesale basis by the RPG-7 in the early 1970s, the RPG-2 was found in use in remote corners of the world by guerrilla groups and some underdeveloped countries' reserve and militia units. However the RPG-2 and its projectiles are no longer produced and few now remain in use. That said, some RPG-2s were still in use with the Taliban in 2010.

## PERFECTION OF A CONCEPT: TOWARD THE RPG-7

In the early 1950s there were three antitank weapon systems available to the infantry platoon: the RPG-2 antitank projector, the VG-45 antitank rifle grenade launched from the AK-47 assault rifle, and the RKG-3 antitank hand grenade. In 1954 a study was undertaken to determine the effectiveness of these weapons and to ascertain whether replacements were necessary. In 1958 the State Committee for Defense Equipment designated the State Specialized Design Bureau – GSKB-47 – in Moscow as the lead enterprise to develop antitank rocket systems. The Rocket Launcher Division of the Engineering Research Institute and elements of other rocket-related research establishments were transferred to GSKB-47. This resulted in the establishment of a rocket launcher research facility at Krasnoarmeysk outside Moscow, complete with firing ranges. Unlike that of the Kalashnikov AK assault rifle, which was the genius of one man (albeit with much technical assistance), the development of subsequent RPG models involved a huge number of designers and engineers.

### The RPG-4

Development of the RPG-2's potential replacement began at GSKB-47 in 1958. This was the RPG-150 (aka RPG-400) and its PG-150 HEAT projectile. A major innovation in this weapon was a small expansion chamber in the 45mm tube. This increased the muzzle velocity and range. It also had a cone-shaped blast deflector to better protect the gunner and accelerate the rearward-flowing propellant gas. Additionally the iron

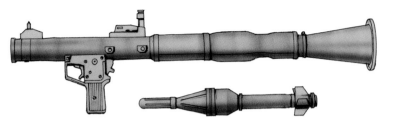

The 1958 experimental 45mm RPG-4 (aka RPG-150 or RPG-400) with its 83mm PG-4 HEAT round. The optical sight is not fitted. The RPG-4 was dropped from development in 1960 in favor of the more advanced RPG-7, which was undergoing simultaneous development. (Drawing by Tony Bryan)

## RPG-4 characteristics

| | | |
|---|---|---|
| Bore caliber | 45mm | 1.77in |
| Warhead caliber | 83mm | 3.27in |
| Launcher length | approx 900mm | 35.43in |
| Projectile length | information not available | |
| Launcher weight | 4.7kg | 10.36lb |
| Projectile weight* | 1.9kg | 4.19lb |
| Muzzle velocity | 84m/s | 275fps |
| Effective range | 300m | 328 yards |
| Armor penetration | 220mm | 8.7in |
| Rate of fire | 4–6rpm | |

*with propellant charge attached

sights were improved and other refinements made. A major improvement was an optical sight which was so advanced that it would be used in the later RPG-7. The same pistol grip, trigger, and ignition system as the RPG-2 was used, as it needed no improvement. The weapon was nearly 2kg heavier than the RPG-2, a significant weight increase as the RPG-2 weighed only 2.86kg. The 83mm HEAT round was also much improved; although it offered only a 20mm penetration increase, its range was doubled over the RPG-2's. It had a separate propellant cartridge that screwed on to the base of the tailboom like the PG-2.

Troop testing of the RPG-150 began in 1958 to determine handling characteristics; further testing and range-firing was undertaken, and it was redesignated the RPG-4 and the projectile the PG-4. The RPG-4 was very similar in design and appearance to the RPG-7, which was concurrently undergoing development. The RPG-4 was 50mm shorter than the RPG-7, had only the trigger pistol grip rather than a second rearward grip, and had a distinct bulge shape for the tube's expansion chamber. While the RPG-7 offered many refinements over the RPG-4, it was the RPG-7's sophisticated PG-7 projectile that led to its adoption in lieu of the RPG-4. RPG-4 development finally ceased in 1960.

The Soviets often concurrently developed competing weapon systems for the same requirements, in case one should fail to meet expectations. This was the case with the RPG-4 and 7, and for that matter possibly the RPG-3 and 5. No information has come to light on either the RPG-3 or 5 weapons and these were probably paper developmental projects. RPG-6 designation was skipped to prevent confusion with the World War II RPG-6 antitank hand grenade.

## The RPG-7

When development of the RPG-2's replacement began in May 1958, the GSKB-47 Design Bureau's goal was to improve the RPG-2 concept and produce a weapon with increased range, greater accuracy, and a more lethal warhead. The lead designer for the RPS-250 was V. K. Firulin. The RPS-250 was adopted as the RPG-7 after extensive testing in 1961, as was the PG-7 HEAT projectile.[3]

To achieve the desired improvements, the Soviets adopted several overlapping concepts and technologies to enhance each aspect, rather than putting in place just a single improvement for each. These enhancements were incorporated into both the launcher and the projectile. For increased range, a lengthy expansion chamber was included in the center of the tube to provide a higher muzzle velocity; a larger primary propellant cartridge was developed with a much improved propellant; a single-grain main rocket motor was incorporated into the tailboom which more than doubled its velocity after launch; and a more ballistically efficient projectile design was developed.

The main improvement in pursuit of greater accuracy was the addition of an optical, telescopic sight, iron sights being retained for backup. A second handgrip was provided for more stable aiming. A long cone-shaped blast deflector was fitted on the breech to narrow the width of the back blast area and to facilitate immediate dispersal to ensure a lack of recoil.

The improvements resulted in a weapon that was slightly over twice the weight of the RPG-2; somewhat bulkier, though shorter; a little more complex to train on and operate; and comparatively more expensive, consuming more time and material to produce both launchers and projectiles. The trade-offs were well worth it. All of the design goals were achieved, with the biggest dividend a three-fold increase in effective range. The Soviets experienced little difficulty in retraining soldiers to use the RPG-7. While a little more complex practically in regard to the sight, it operated in much the same manner as its predecessor; pistol grip, trigger, and safety were identical. The bore and inside of the blast deflector were chrome-plated to prolong barrel life and make cleaning easier. In 1962 the establishments responsible for the RPG-7's design were awarded the Lenin Prize for Technology.

The RPG-7V was introduced in 1970 and was designed to accept night vision sights. The East Germans and Poles designated it the RPG-7W, but it was in fact the same weapon, not a different model. There was also an RPG-7V1 with a detachable folding bipod at the muzzle. As a practical measure most parts were interchangeable among the RPG-7, RPG-7V, and RPG-7V1. There were no differences in capability and RPG-7V and RPG-7V1 characteristics are the same as those of the RPG-7. The ability to fit a night vision sight on the RPG-7V and RPG-7V1 versions provided

---

[3] The RPG-7 is known by the GRAU designation of "6G3" (GRAU = Main Agency of Missiles and Artillery of the Ministry of Defense) and the projectile as the "7P1." These are administrative numbers.

## RPG-7 characteristics

| | | |
|---|---|---|
| Bore caliber | 40mm | 1.57in |
| Warhead caliber: | | |
| PG-7 | 85mm | 3.35in |
| PG-7M | 70mm | 2.76in |
| Launcher length | 950mm | 37.40in |
| Projectile length*: | | |
| PG-7 | 899mm | 35.39in |
| PG-7M | 951mm | 37.44in |
| Launcher weight | 2.86kg | 6.31lb |
| Projectile weight*: | | |
| PG-7 | 2.25kg | 4.96lb |
| PG-7M | 1.84kg | 4.05lb |
| Muzzle velocity: | | |
| PG-7 | 117m/s | 384fps |
| PG-7M | 140m/s | 459fps |
| Effective range | 150m | 164 yards |
| Armor penetration: | | |
| PG-7 | 260mm | 10.2in |
| PG-7M | 300mm | 11.8in |
| Rate of fire | 4–6rpm | |

Note: PG-7M projectile introduced in 1969

*with propellant charge attached

A Soviet soldier firing an RPG-7, showing the weapon's distinctive firing signature. Crews were trained to move immediately to another firing position before firing again. (© Dmitri Baltermants/The Dmitri Baltermants Collection/Corbis)

# RPG-7 CUTAWAY

## The RPG-7V exposed

The RPG-7V is a remarkably simple weapon; its most complex components are its ammunition and optical sight. Simplicity means low cost, rapid production, ease of maintenance in the field, ease of training and operation, and, most importantly, high reliability and lethality.

1. Projectile alignment notch
2. Front iron sight
3. Forward sling swivel
4. Rear iron sight
5. Expansion chamber (enlarged barrel section)
6. Chrome-plated bore
7. The barrel is assembled from two sections, but cannot be field-disassembled
8. Rear sling swivel
9. Back blast deflection cone (chrome-plated)
10. Trigger
11. Safety stud
12. Hammer cocking piece (cannot be seen)
13. Optical sight mount
14. PGO-7VZ 2.5x optical sight
15. Sight reticle lamp for night firing

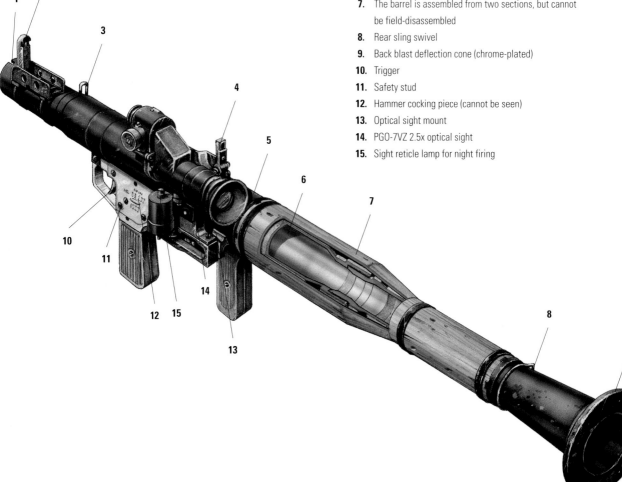

## RPG-7 ammunition

A wide variety of ammunition is available for the RPG-7 and is made in a number of countries. This is a mere sampling. Not all are merely copies of standard Soviet/Russian-designed rounds; some are of indigenous design. Most projectiles are olive drab or olive green with black markings. Training rounds are black. Propellant charges are not shown attached on these rounds. An RPG-2's (1) and RPG-16's (14) projectiles are included for comparison. The warhead's caliber is indicated in parentheses along with its weight.

1. Soviet PG-2 HEAT (80mm, 1.84kg)
2. Soviet PG-7 HEAT (85mm, 2.25kg)
3. Soviet PG-7M HEAT (70mm, 1.98kg)
4. Soviet PG-7L HEAT (93mm, 2.6kg)
5. Soviet PG-7R tandem HEAT (105mm, 4.5kg)
6. Russian TBG-7 thermobaric (105mm, 4.5kg)
7. Russian OG-7 HE/frag (40mm, 1.76kg)
8. Russian OG-7V HE/frag (40mm, 2kg)
9. Iranian NAFEZ HEAT (80mm, 1.52kg)
10. Slovakian PG-7M 110 HEAT (110mm, 3.15kg)
11. Chinese Type II HEAT (94mm, 2.8kg)
12. Chinese Type III (80mm, 2.26kg)
13. Chinese airburst HE/frag (75mm, 2.62kg)
14. PG-16 HEAT (65mm, 2.05kg)

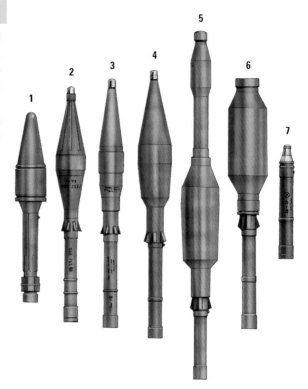

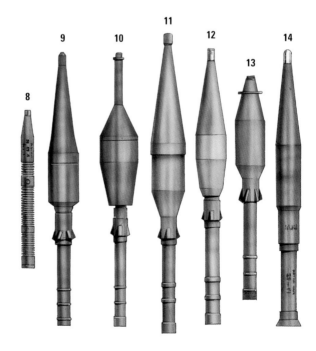

An RPG-7D issued to Soviet and
Warsaw Pact airborne forces
and *Spetznaz* until replaced
by the RPG-16. This illustration
from a Soviet training chart
shows it both assembled and
broken down for jumping. The
upper right insert diagrams show
the linkage rod that blocks the
hammer when the weapon is
broken down to prevent it from
being fired without the rear barrel
section coupled.

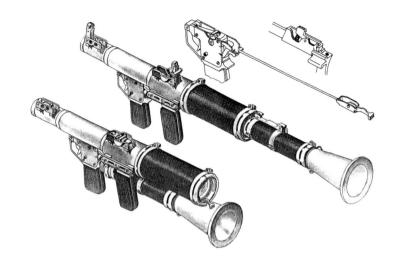

it with a 24-hour-a-day capability (described below). The PGO-7V optical sight supplied with the RPG-7V1 has an improved reticle to increase accuracy, and was introduced in the late 1980s with the PGO-7VZ sight to accommodate the longer-ranged rounds introduced then. A final version was the RPG-7V2 which added the UP-7V range device, allowing up to 700m for the TBG-7 thermobaric and OG-7 HE/frag rounds.

The RPG-7's nickname is sometimes said to be the *Knut* (Knout),[4] but this is not confirmed as official and the name appears to be little used by troops. If it is actually a nickname it appears not to have been bestowed until the 1990s. The RPG-7V is currently manufactured in Russia by the Kovrov Mechanical Plant, Kovrov, Vladimar Region and it is marketed by Bazalt State Research and Production Enterprise in Moscow. Other firms have manufactured all variants of the RPG-7.

### The RPG-7D

The RPG-7D was introduced for airborne troops in 1968 (D for *Desantnii* – paratrooper). When first observed by NATO it was given the tentative designation of "RPG-8," and it was soon followed by the RPG-7D1, which could accept a night vision sight. The RPG-7D2 mounted the PGO-7VZ sight for longer-ranged rounds.

The RPG-7D could be broken down into two sections for packing in a parachute jump container and for non-tactical carrying. The rear section of the barrel, behind the expansion chamber, separated from the forward section by means of a three-lug bayonet joint. The rear section could be attached underneath the forward section by means of a latch device fitted on the upper forward end of the rear section. In order to prevent the RPG-7D from being fired without the rear section attached, an internal linkage rod connected a latch on the lower rear end of the forward section to the hammer in the forward pistol grip. Without the rear section attached the linkage rod was held forward, blocking the hammer. When the rear section was attached the

---

[4] A *knut* is a flogging whip made of braided rawhide thongs, sometimes with wire or hooks incorporated, attached to a wood handle.

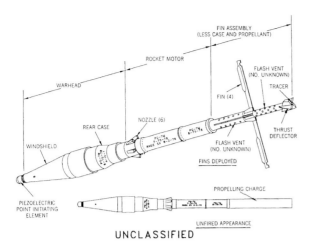

The details of the improved 70mm PG-7M HEAT projectile introduced in 1969. This is the round most commonly used in the RPG-7 today.

linkage rod was released, allowing the hammer to be cocked. The RPG-7D's characteristics were basically the same as the RPG-7's, but it weighed 7.4kg and was 945mm in length assembled. The RPG-7D1 was 950mm long assembled and 655mm when broken down. Over 80 percent of the replacement parts were interchangeable between the RPG-7 and 7D.

## The RPG-7 technical specifications and improvements

The RPG-7 has a large expansion chamber in its 40mm barrel, and approximately the rear half of the barrel covered by a wooden sheath extending from the rear grip to the cone-shaped blast deflector. Newer models have phenolic-impregnated[5] laminated wooden shields and the Chinese use phenolic shields. The trigger grip is the same as the RPG-2's.

A significant improvement over the RPG-2 is the PGO-7 optical sight, which is attached to the left side of the launcher between the two handgrips. The sight weighs 0.5kg and is a 2.7× reflex sight with a 13-degree field of vision. Yellow and green lens filters are provided to adapt it to different lighting and haze conditions. The sight reticle has three separate stadia and line sets: range estimation stadia at 100m intervals (200–1,000m) set for a 2.7m high target (the average height of a tank falls between Soviet tanks at 2.3m and US tanks at 3m), range lines at 100m intervals (200–500m), and lead and crosswind correction lines at 10-mil intervals (1–5), plus a bore sighting mark (+).[6] A small battery-powered lamp can be attached to the sight to illuminate the sight reticle at night. In some references it is inferred that this provides a night vision capability, but it does not; the lamp merely allows the sight stadia and lines to be seen against a dark target or sight picture background. There still must be sufficient moonlight, starlight, or other external illumination to make the target visible to the gunner. The lamp uses a small SM-2 bulb and the 5 V/0.075 A bzw. SM-36 battery.

---

[5] Phenolic resin is a Bakelite- or plastic-like heat-resistant synthetic material.
[6] There are 6,000 Russian mils in a 360-degree circle as opposed to 6,400 Western mils. One Russian mil equals approximately 16.6 degrees while one Western mil equals approximately 18 degrees in angle. References here are to Russian mils.

The new projectile's design improved accuracy through its higher velocity and much-improved fins, and also the incorporation of a more effective shaped-charge design. Besides the copper cone lining there is an aluminum trumpet-shaped liner in the nosecone. This helps focus the explosive blast into a more concentrated penetrating jet. A point-initiating, base-detonating fuze is used with a piezoelectric element in the nose. When it strikes the target it initiates an electrical connection through the warhead's outer body, which is in contact with the VL-7M base-detonating fuze. The fuze also contains a pyrotechnic element and detents for arming and safety functions. A set-back igniter, self-destruct element, and spring-loaded shutter containing a spark-gap detonator serve to initiate self-destruction. The warhead will self-destruct – detonate – approximately 4.8 seconds after firing at a range of 920m.[7]

While spin-stabilized shaped-charge projectiles do not achieve as much penetration as fin-stabilized – owing to the blast's dispersal by centrifugal force – the PG-7's fins imparted only a very slow (ten rotations per second) counterclockwise spin for improved accuracy. It is often stated that the RPG-7 is greatly affected by crosswinds, as the projectile will slightly turn into a crosswind. A 10kph (6.2mph) crosswind will allow for only a

[7] Early PG-2 projectiles and many special-purpose RPG-7 projectiles lack the self-destruct feature.

## RPG-7 FIRING SEQUENCE

### Stage 1

The assistant gunner attaches the propellant charge to the projectile as the gunner removes the muzzle and breech caps, and optical sight lens cover, and checks the bore for obstructions.

### Stage 2

The assistant passes the ready projectile to the gunner.

50 percent first hit probability at beyond 180m. While a fully trained gunner is taught to compensate for this, the variables make this only partly effective. Most insurgents and less well-trained troops are even less effective. However, this fault is not unique to the RPG-7; it applies to any fin-stabilized rocket launcher including the M72 LAW, AT4, and others.[8] There is a common misunderstanding of how the RPG-7's propellant system operates. It consists of two elements. The first is a propellant or launching cartridge that is carried separately and screwed on to the end of the tailboom prior to firing. This is often referred to incorrectly as a "booster." It is a waterproof resin-covered cardboard tube containing a 264mm tube to which four long blade-type fins are attached. These are hinged and folded forward. At the end of the rod is a knob-like fitting containing the red-burning tracer, with four tiny fins intended to impart a counterclockwise spin before the larger fins deploy.

In the end of the projectile's tailboom, to which the propelling cartridge is attached, is the percussion primer which is ignited by the RPG's firing pin when the trigger is pulled. This ignites the propellant charge and activates the ZV-7G delay element just forward of the primer in the tailboom.

[8] In contrast to that provided to Russian gunners, little training is given to US soldiers on how to estimate and counter crosswinds when using the LAW; in fact it is seldom mentioned as a problem during LAW training and is not addressed in US manuals.

**Stage 3**

The projectile is loaded, ensuring the indexing pin is properly seated in the notch atop the barrel at the muzzle. The assistant prepares the next round.

**Stage 4**

The gunner shoulders the weapon, cocks it, and takes it off safe. The gunner takes aim and fires the weapon. The assistant gunner provides supporting small arms fire.

When fired the launcher cartridge propels the projectile out of the barrel at 117m/s. At 11m from the muzzle the delay element ignites the rocket charge contained in the tailboom, boosting the velocity to 294m/s. The propellant charge is a hollow cylinder. The propellant burns *forward* and vents through six wedge-shaped lugs at the forward end of the tailboom just below the base of the warhead. These vents are angled 18 degrees outward, and being near the projectile's center of gravity help stabilize it and create a torque opposite of the rotation imparted by the fins to reduce spin rate. This is more of a "booster" charge than the launching charge.

The original PG-7 projectile was 85mm, with a length of 899mm, and had flutes stamped in the nosecone. In 1969 the designer V. I. Medvedev developed a new HEAT projectile, the PG-7M (*Modernizirovanii –* Modernized). It was 70mm in caliber and 52mm longer than the original. Rather than being fluted, the nosecone had a smooth, streamlined appearance. It left the launcher at a higher velocity, but reached the same velocity as the PG-7.[9] It was lighter, more accurate and reliable, less affected by wind, and had an improved VP-7M fuze and up to 40mm more penetration. The PG-7M was fielded throughout the 1970s, but is still encountered to this day. Regardless of newer improved rounds that have since become available, the PG-7M is the most common. Its impact is impressive, penetrating 0.46m of reinforced concrete and 1.52m of earth and logs.

Other new rounds were the improved 72mm PG-7S, which entered service in 1972, and the 93mm PG-7L, with much improved armor penetration, which was introduced in 1977. It could penetrate 600mm of armor, 1.1m of reinforced concrete, 1.5m of brick, and 2.5m of logs and earth. The 105mm PG-7R tandem warhead HEAT round was adopted in 1988 in an effort to defeat explosive reactive armor (ERA). It is expensive and to date few have appeared on battlefields. The idea of the tandem warhead is that it has a small shaped-charge on the end of an extender ahead of the main shaped-charge. The small charge will cut a small hole into the armor, though not penetrating. The main charge will follow through the "starter-hole." With ERA the small charge will detonate ERA

[9] Often seen as "PG-7V." "V" simply means the propellant charge is attached; thus the PG-7 and PG-7V are the same.

bricks and should allow the main charge to penetrate undisturbed by the bricks' detonation. Likewise it will cut a hole through chain-link, slat-armor, or appliqué armor, allowing the main charge to hit the main armor. The PG-7R can penetrate 600mm of armor, 1.5m of reinforced concrete and masonry, and 2.7m of earth and logs. The impact of the PG-7LT round is similar, but has slightly greater penetration.

Four models of night vision sights may be attached to the RPG-7. These include the NSP-2 infrared sight and the PGN-1, 1PN58, and 1LH52 image intensifier sights. The attachment of night vision sights adds to the launcher's weight and unbalances the weapon, making it more awkward to handle. The outdated NSP-2 was an active IR sight that could be detected by other IR sights, metascopes (passive IR receivers), and passive image intensifier sights. The gunner could see only directly down the beam. There was no "glow" to the sides to allow him to see targets or movement outside the beam as with a visible light beam. Instead, looking down an IR beam was like looking down a tunnel. The NSP-2 weighed 6kg and had a 150–200m range under ideal conditions. Few if any NSP-2s remain in use. The PGN-1 image intensifier sight of 1969 is similar in design to the NSP-3 used on small arms (assault rifles, sniper rifles, light machine guns), but it was designed for the RPG-7. The 1PN58 image intensifier sight is similar to the PGN-1 with minor improvements. The PGN-1 and 1PN58 are first-generation image intensifiers with long tubular sights, weighing around 3.5kg with a 3.4× magnification. The second-generation 1LH52 weighs 3.2kg with a 5.3× magnification. Passive image intensifier sights – "starlight scopes" – enhance available light and cannot be detected by other devices. They have an effective viewing range of 400m. One PGN-1 or 1PN58 sight is generally issued per platoon in priority units, allowing one of its three RPG-7s to be so fitted.

An Afghanistan National Army soldier fires an RPG-7, demonstrating the degree of concussion and blast caused by its firing. The RPG-7 has remained a standard weapon in the new army along with other Russian-origin weapons. (US Army/Spc Daniel Love)

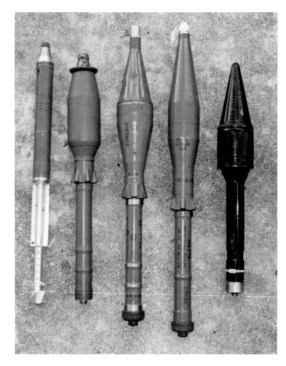

The PUS-7 sub-caliber device was developed in 1962 as a low-cost training device. Czechoslovakia later produced a similar version. It is externally similar to the PG-7 projectile, other than being printed yellow, and has a muzzle opening in the nose. This device contains a horizontal firing pin activated by the RPG-7's vertical firing pin to fire a 7.62x39mm tracer cartridge (green tip), the same as that used in AK-47 assault rifles. The cartridge is loaded into the device by twisting and pulling back on a sleeve on the tailboom. This exposes a rectangular opening and a cartridge is inserted into the chamber; the sleeve is pushed forward and twisted, and a latch locks it. The device itself is loaded into the muzzle of the RPG-7 in the same manner as a projectile. After firing, the device is removed and

reloaded. This provides training to both the gunner and assistant gunner as he rapidly reloads the launcher. But it does not provide experience in realistic reload rates owing to the need to first remove and reload the just-fired device, unless multiple devices are available. While the trajectory is similar to that of the PG-7 projectile, it provides no means of compensating for the actual projectile's crosswind drift. Nor does it provide any sensation of back blast impulse or the noise signature.

## The RPG-7's combat debut

The RPG-7's first combat use was by the Egyptians in the 1967 Arab–Israeli War. It was employed to a limited extent at that time, but saw much greater use in the 1973 and subsequent wars. Israel captured such large qualities of RPG-7s from Egypt and Syria that she issued them to selected units. The RPG-7 was first encountered by the US in Vietnam in late 1967, but it did not see widespread use until early 1968. Unlike the RPG-2, the RPG-7 proved to be effective against American M48A3 tanks in Vietnam. It could also penetrate bunkers, masonry buildings, and other fortifications more effectively than the RPG-2, and the terminal effect of the projectile's warhead inside the target was more lethal. Although the projectile's tendency to turn slightly into a crosswind was an evident problem, even in the hands of the most unskilled Viet Cong it was a formidable weapon.

# The RPG-16

A special antitank weapon for airborne troops, the RPG-16 was developed in 1968 by the GSKB-47 Design Bureau under designer I. E. Rogozin. Adopted in 1970, it was first seen in 1976 parades being carried by paratroopers, and was provisionally dubbed the "RPG-9" by NATO intelligence. It was soon redesignated the "RPG-16D" by NATO as it broke down into two sections like the RPG-7D, for packing in airdrop containers and for transport inside the cramped BMD-1 combat vehicle, an air-droppable, full-tracked fighting vehicle used by Soviet/Russian airborne forces.

## RPG-16 characteristics

| | | |
|---|---|---|
| Bore caliber | 58.3mm | 2.3in |
| Warhead caliber | 65.2mm | 2.6in |
| Launcher length | 1,104mm | 43.46in |
| Projectile length* | 980mm | 38.58in |
| Launcher weight | 10.3kg | 22.7lb |
| Projectile weight | 2.05kg | 4.51lb |
| Muzzle velocity | 130m/s | 427fps |
| Effective range | 800m | 875 yards |
| Armor penetration | 300mm | 11.8in |
| Rate of fire | 5–6rpm | |

*with propellant charge attached

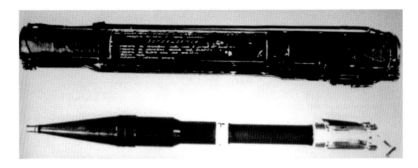

The RPG-18 *Muhka* (Fly) antitank rocket, the first of the Soviet single-shot, disposable RPGs, is shown in its stowed (not extended) launch tube, along with a 64mm PG-18 HEAT rocket. (US DoD)

## Other RPGs

Besides the reloadable RPG-2, 7, and 16 there are a number of other shoulder-fired weapons designated "RPG."

| | |
|---|---|
| RPG-18 *Mukha* | 64mm single-shot, copy of US M72 LAW, *c.* 1975 |
| RPG-22 *Netto* | 73mm single-shot, 1985 |
| RPG-26 *Aglen* | 73mm, improved RPG-22, *c.* 1990 |
| RPG-27 *Tavolga* | 105mm, enlarged RPG-26, tandem warhead, 1992 |
| RPG-29 *Vampir* | 105mm, heavy breech-reloadable, 1989 |
| RPG-30 | 105mm upgraded RPG-27 with 30mm "precursor rocket," 2009 |
| RPG-32 *Hashim* | 105mm, breech-reloadable, 2007 |
| RPG-75 *Kobilka* | 68mm, single-shot, Czechoslovakia, 1980 |
| RPG-76 *Komar* | 68mm, single-shot, Poland, 1995 |
| RShG-1* | 105mm, RPG-27 with thermobaric warhead, 2001 |
| RShG-2* | 73mm, RPG-26 with thermobaric warhead, 2001 |

* RShG = (rocket grenade, assault).

It was expected that an "RPG-16" non-breakdown version would appear at any time within motorized rifle units as a replacement for the RPG-7. However, this never materialized. As far as can be determined the weapon was designated only as the RPG-16 with no "D" even if it was a paratrooper's breakdown weapon. The RPG-16 was larger and more robust than the RPG-7 and was eventually nicknamed the *Grom* (Thunder).

It is thought that this heavier and more capable weapon was issued to paratroopers to provide them with a more substantial antiarmor capability at the smallest tactical subunit level. Such a high density of longer-ranged weapons, i.e. one per squad, would also make up for fewer heavier antiarmor weapons at company and battalion levels. The RPG-16, though, was significantly heavier – weighing about one and a half times as much as the RPG-7D – and more complex, and it used an electrical firing system. This made it a less than ideal weapon for airborne troops in some regards. It is speculated that it was intended to replace both the RPG-7D and the much heavier and bulkier 73mm SPG-9 *Kopye* recoilless gun in airborne units; otherwise its use makes little sense. It is believed that 116,883 had been produced by 1999, but that it is no longer in production.

The RPG-16 was issued only to Soviet/Russian airborne and *Spetznaz* units. None ever appeared in other Warsaw Pact airborne units, nor was it exported until after the USSR's fall. It is used by some now independent former USSR states as well as Afghanistan, and possibly other countries. The RPG-16 saw its first combat during the Soviet invasion of Afghanistan where it was found to be effective against fortified positions because of its better accuracy and improved warhead.

## The RPG-16 technical specifications and improvements

While the operating principle of the RPG-16 is similar to that of the RPG-7, there are many differences. It is of larger caliber, 58.3mm, but employs only a slightly larger 65.2mm warhead. It has only a single trigger grip and a small forward horizontal handgrip, while a folding bipod is fitted behind the muzzle. A major difference is that the RPG-16 uses an electrical firing system rather than a percussion-type hammer. It has a lever-like safety switch on the left side of the trigger grip. Forward is fire and rearward is safe. The RPG-16 has a chrome-plated bore and blast cone.

The 2.7× PGO-16 sight includes a reticle lighting lamp and is similar in design to the RPG-7's PGO-7, but the sight reticle is graduated very differently. The PGN-1, 1PN58, and 1LH52 image intensifier sights may be fitted in place of the optical sight. Folding iron sights similar to those on the RPG-7 are provided.

The weapon can be broken down into two sections like the RPG-7D. A bayonet joint connection is located at the forward end of the heat guard. The two sections can be fastened together for non-tactical carrying in a single unit and the weapon is fitted with a trigger block to prevent firing in the disassembled state. The rear barrel section has an expansion chamber.

The RPG-16 is loaded from the muzzle. The PG-16V HEAT projectile's design is improved over those used with the RPG-7. It is more akin to the PG-9 projectile used with the 73mm SPG-9 recoilless gun. The streamlined 65mm warhead has a tailboom that contains a booster rocket with six short folding knife-type tailfins. A PG-16R primary propellant cartridge is screwed on to the fin assembly. The round is often described as being a "tandem warhead," but it is not. Once loaded, the firing sequence is much the same as with the RPG-7 except for electrical ignition. The PG-16V projectile leaves the muzzle at 130m/s and achieves a velocity of 350m/s when the booster rocket ignites approximately 12m from the muzzle. The fins located behind the rocket charge's exhaust nozzle reduce crosswind effects. There is also an HE/frag projectile, possibly the OG-16. Both have a self-destruct capability and tracer.

## RPG accessories

Regardless of the model, RPGs have been issued with a number of accessories, the design and type varying by model and also by country of manufacture. These include ammunition backpacks for gunners and assistant gunners: the gunners hold two projectiles and propellant charges plus spare parts, cleaning and maintenance tools, while the assistants hold three projectiles and charges. Charges are not normally attached to the tailboom until ready for firing, but in combat it is not uncommon to see rounds with the charges attached protruding from backpacks or rucksacks. The backpacks may be made of canvas or vinyl-coated synthetic fabrics. Carrying slings can be made of leather or webbing and often have muzzle and breech covers of the same materials attached by cords or thin straps. For optical sights a pouch is issued, containing spare sight illumination bulbs and batteries.

## RPG spin-offs and non-Russian variants

Numerous license-built versions and reverse-engineered knock-offs of the RPG-2 and 7 have been built, as well as other weapons based on the systems. In particular, several countries have either license-built or reverse-engineered the RPG-7, developing identical or very close copies. In addition, countries producing RPG-7s also produce ammunition, sometimes including advanced designs, often of their own origin.

### China

Hizbul Islam militiamen in Somalia load a Chinese Type 69-I with its standard folding bipod attached. These bipods are seldom-used, and if they are fitted, users will more often than not remove them to reduce the weight and bulk. (Mohamed Dahir/AFP/Getty Images)

To replace the outdated Type 56 (RPG-2) the Chinese reverse-engineered the RPG-7 in the early 1960s and test-fired it in 1964, but did not standardize it until 1969 as the Type 69. Production began in 1970 and it was first seen in 1972. The Type 69 did not see use in Vietnam, but was employed in the 1979 Sino–Vietnam border conflict both against personnel and to breach obstacles.

## Chinese Type 69-I characteristics

| | | |
|---|---|---|
| Bore caliber | 40mm | 1.57in |
| Warhead caliber | 80mm | 3.15in |
| Launcher length | 910mm | 35.8in |
| Projectile length* | 926mm | 36.46in |
| Launcher weight | 5.6kg | 12.35lb |
| Projectile weight* | 2.1kg | 4.63lb |
| Muzzle velocity | 120m/s | 393fps |
| Effective range | 500m | 545 yards |
| Armor penetration | 150mm | 6in |
| Rate of fire | 4–6rpm | |
| *with propellant charge attached | | |

The Chinese sight reticle is very different from the Russian. There are two sets of stadia lines for estimating range via tank height. The right scale is for Russian tanks (2.3m) and the left for US (3m), unlike the Russian sight stadia which are set for an average height of 2.7m. The Chinese sight also has simplified, yet improved, crosswind correction stadia lines. It will not fit on Soviet RPG-7s.

The improved Type 69-I was introduced in the mid-1980s by China North Industries Corporation (NORINCO) in Beijing. While outwardly similar to the Type 69, it offers many refinements and minor improvements. The barrel is a little shorter, but it is heavier than the Type 69. The heat guard, pistol grips, and carrying handle are made of a reddish-brown composite material providing more efficient heat insulation than wood. The carrying handle is fitted to the rear of the optical sight mount. The rear handgrip is slightly further back, just behind the forward end of the heat guard instead of just forward of it. The Type 69 2.5× sight is simplified over the PGO-7 and the rear iron sight is adjustable for windage, a feature not found on its Soviet counterparts. A folding bipod is attached behind the front iron sight. The Chinese fielded a range of nine different projectiles. The Chinese-made Type I and Type II infrared night sights and Type II image intensifier sight can be fitted on the Type 69-I. The Type 69-I is widely exported, but has begun to be replaced in Chinese service by the 80mm PF-89 shoulder-fired disposable rocket launcher, although it still remains in use.

### Egypt, Pakistan, and Iraq

In the mid-1970s, Egypt, which had been using Soviet-supplied RPG-7s since 1966, reverse-engineered the RPG-7 and began producing its own as the PG-7 in the Sakr Factory for Developed Industries, Cairo, as the Soviets no longer supplied RPG-7s or other weapons after the failure of the 1973 Yom Kippur War. The PG-7 is virtually identical to the Soviet RPG-7. The PG-7 is marketed for export and is also marketed as the "home guard antipersonnel weapon." This is nothing more than a PG-7 launcher coupled with a special HE/frag round.

Three homemade Iraqi insurgent RPG-type rocket launchers captured by US Marines and Iraqi Special Forces in Fallujah in 2004. These launchers used light alloy or even PVC tubes and were good for only a few rounds before they became hazardous. To the left are a 7.62mm RPK (light machine gun version of the AKM assault rifle with its butt stock missing) and an RPG-7V antitank weapon. (US Marine Corps/SSgt Jonathan C. Knauth)

An exact copy of the Soviet RPG-7 is produced in Pakistan under license and is used by the Pakistani Army. It is offered for export sale by the Pakistan Machine Tool Factory Ltd., Landhi. While the characteristics are the same, the performance data provided by the manufacturer is slightly different from the Soviet version.

The Al-Nassira is an exact copy of the Soviet RPG-7 produced under license since the early 1980s by Iraq. The main difference is that a simple detachable mechanical tangent sight is provided rather than an optical sight. PGO-7-type sights cannot be mounted on the Al-Nassira. The weapon's other characteristics are identical to those of the RPG-7, but it is slightly lighter as it lacks the sight. Iraq has also used large numbers of Soviet-made RPG-7s and possibly Chinese-made models.

After the 2003 US invasion of Iraq very crude RPG-like weapons were fabricated in machine shops using steel tubes, simple percussion firing systems, strapped-on wooden grips, and iron sights. They could fire RPG-7 projectiles, but were often hazardous to the firer.

### Iran

In Iran, the Armament Industries Group, Defense Industries Organization license-produces the *Sageg*, an RPG-7 virtually identical to the Russian one, but with a simplified optical sight. There is also a "commando" version with a shortened barrel. Iran also uses Soviet and other Warsaw Pact-made RPG-7s and probably possesses Chinese Type 69-Is. The Iranian Revolutionary Guard employed multiple mountings of four or six RPG-7s aboard high-speed boats to harass tankers during the 1984–86 Persian Gulf Tanker War. Other innovative uses can be expected around the world.

A Polish soldier armed with a Polish-made RPG-7W rushes forward with his squad. The RPG crew would be positioned in the center of the squad line formation adjacent to the squad leader for ease of control. The RPG was not to be fired unless ordered by the squad leader.

## Eastern Europe

Warsaw Pact license-built RPG-7s were identical to the Soviet models. They were manufactured in Bulgaria (RPG-7V) by Kintex, by Czechoslovakia (RPG-7, RPG-7V *Pancéřovka* – antitank weapon),[10] East Germany (RPG-7, RPG-7W – often referred to as a *Panzerbüchse* – anti-armor weapon), Poland (RPG-7, RPG-7W), and Romania (RPG-7V, RPG-7D). The Romanian weapons produced by Romtechnica have a folding bipod fixed to the muzzle. Note that the East German and Polish RPG-7Ws were identical to the Soviet RPG-7V. Only Bulgaria and Romania have exported their own variants.

The East German AGI 3x40 incendiary grenade projector (*Brandgranatenwerfer*) is arguably the most unusual of the RPG variants. It was first publicized in 1982, but was not adopted by the East German Army until 1987. It was issued only to the 1st Motorized Rifle Division stationed outside East Berlin with the wartime mission of seizing West Berlin. It was not exported and most were destroyed after reunification. This launcher was intended for firing incendiary rockets at buildings, fortifications, and light AFVs; no antiarmor rounds were available.

The meaning of "AGI" is unknown, but "3x40" refers to its three 40mm barrels arranged at 120-degree points of a circle. The barrels were mounted on a bipod attached to the forward barrel-mounting bracket just behind the muzzles. An optical sight was fitted to the side of the left barrel, as was the trigger grip. The grip contained a 5-volt, 1-amp electric capacitor that ignited the rockets' propelling charges. The 2.7× sight had an integral lamp to illuminate the sight reticle. The optical sight weighed 1.3kg.

[10] From the late 1950s and into the 1980s Czechoslovakia used the P27 *Pancéřovka* (45mm barrel, 120mm warhead), superficially similar to the RPG-2. It was replaced by the RPG-7 in the 1980s.

## East German AGI 3x40 characteristics

| | | |
|---|---|---|
| Bore caliber | 40mm | 1.57in |
| Warhead caliber | 72mm | 2.83in |
| Launcher length | 958mm | 37.7in |
| Projectile length | 603mm | 23.7in |
| Launcher weight | 11kg+ | 24lb+ |
| Projectile weight | 2.25kg | 4.96lb |
| Muzzle velocity | 90m/s | 295fps |
| Effective range | 200m | 220 yards |
| Indirect fire | 550m | 600 yards |
| Rate of fire | 6rpm (3rpm sustained) | |

The barrels were loaded with incendiary rockets, the launcher sighted, and the three rockets fired in sequence with repeated trigger squeezes within two seconds. There was no booster charge. The rocket warheads burst upon impact with a flaming flash and the liquid incendiary filler burned at 1,500–2,000°C (2,732–3,632°F).

The projectile looked like a PG-7M HEAT warhead with an impact-detonated nose fuze mated to a PG-2 tailboom. The ZG2R could not be fired from the RPG-2 or 7 and nor could PG-2 or 7 projectiles be fired from the AGI. This was due to the fact that the alignment studs on the ZG2R rockets were much larger than on RPG projectiles.

### North Vietnam

The B50 was a North Vietnamese-made scaled-up B40 (RPG-2) fielded in about 1966. This little-known crude weapon saw only limited use. It used the same trigger grip and firing system as the B40. A non-folding, adjustable monopod with screw-type elevation was fitted just forward of the trigger grip. Well to the rear was a folding bipod. This allowed the heavier weapon to be fired from the ground as well as from the shoulder. From just to the rear of the trigger grip running back to the bipod was a wooden tube protector. A short flared blast deflector was fitted to the breech. It had folding iron sights graduated to 150m and no optical sight. Its significantly heavier weight and the fact that it offered penetration little better than the B40 made it unpopular. The introduction of the much more effective and lighter RPG-7 in 1967 sealed the B50's fate.

A US Army sketch of the rare North Vietnamese 50mm B50, a scaled-up and overly heavy and bulky version of the B40 (RPG-2) with its 100mm HEAT projectile loaded. Muzzle and breech covers are attached to the weapon. (US Army)

## North Vietnamese B50 characteristics

| | | |
|---|---|---|
| Bore caliber | 50mm | 1.96in |
| Warhead caliber | 100mm | 3.93in |
| Launcher length | 1,321mm | 52in |
| Projectile length* | 1,041mm | 40.98in |
| Launcher weight | 11.7kg | 25.79lb |
| Projectile weight* | 4.5kg | 9.92lb |
| Effective range | 150m | 164 yards |
| Armor penetration | 230mm | 9in |
| Rate of fire | 3–4rpm | |

*with propellant charge attached

## USA

The most recent non-Russian RPG-7 is undergoing redesign by Airtronic USA, Inc. of Elk Grove Village, Illinois and the program was announced in January 2009. It will be a completely reengineered weapon fitted with Picatinny rails that accommodate a variety of sights and night vision devices, an M16-type trigger grip, and an M4 carbine-type shoulder rest. The American RPG-7-USA will be available for purchase through the US Government by countries such as Iraq and Afghanistan, which are reequipping with new Russian-style weapons.

The American-made RPG-7-USA is not yet in series production. It is completely reengineered, along with its ammunition. It uses an M16 rifle-type trigger grip and M4 carbine shoulder rest and is fitted with a laser sight. Any type of standard US sight and night vision device may be mounted. (Airtronic USA)

# USE
## From the Vietnam hills to the streets of Baghdad

The RPG was first and foremost a light antitank weapon allocated to infantry at a platoon level. Although it was never likely to defeat modern main battle tanks with frontal shots, tactics were developed to engage the flanks, rear, and other vulnerable points, and RPGs are undoubtedly effective against lighter AFVs, soft-skin vehicles, buildings, and field fortifications. Since the 1970s specialized and improved projectiles have been developed to allow harder targets to be attacked, as well as to provide special-purpose munitions for purposes such as bunker-bursting, antipersonnel, incendiary, and illumination. Other warheads have also been developed in an effort to defeat ERA and modern advanced armor.

While they are still mainly considered antitank weapons, since the start of the Vietnam War the various RPGs in existance have been used in many innovative ways and against targets never envisioned by their developers. The RPG's light weight, compactness, and simplicity of operation, and the fact that it is so potent for its size, make it readily useable for many different purposes, while its users' fertile imaginations have made it a much more effective and versatile weapon than it appears on the surface.

Conventional armies, including the US, have often underestimated the effects and impact of this simple little weapon. More concerns have been expressed over guided antiarmor missiles and man-portable, shoulder-fired air defense missiles over the years than have ever been voiced about the RPG-7, yet the US has lost more AFVs, transport vehicles, aircraft, and personnel to the RPG-7 than to high-tech guided missiles. Some reports claim that 50 percent of US casualties in the recent conflict in Iraq were caused by RPGs. While this may be inflated, it cannot be disputed that they have certainly caused a high percentage of casualties.

Numbers are not available, but hundreds of AFVs, up-armored Humvees, and other vehicles have been destroyed in Afghanistan and Iraq by RPGs, second only to improvised explosive devices (IEDs) and mines. Only a few have been identified as struck by advanced guided missiles. A few M1A2 Abrams tanks were temporarily disabled by multiple RPG-7 hits in the tracks and road wheels in 2003 and 2004. In 2004 an M1A1 tank was penetrated through the side by an unidentified HEAT warhead, which some claim was an RPG-7, but others suspect to have been an RPG-22, RPG-29, or another weapon. The tank was not actually disabled, but it was pulled out of service for investigation. In the generation prior to the Abrams, a single PG-7M HEAT round had an approximately 40 percent chance of disabling a US M60A3 or M48A5 tank, but only a 5 percent chance of completely destroying it. While RPGs may be even less effective against the current generation of heavy tanks, they can nevertheless inflict a great deal of damage.

A Liberian militiaman fires an RPG-7 at rebel forces in the capital, Monrovia, 2003. (Chris Hondros/Getty Images)

A US soldier watches a Medium Tactical Vehicle Replacement (MTVR) burn after being struck by an RPG-7 round. RPGs of various types proved to be one of the major threat weapons in Iraq. (US Army/SSgt Jeffrey A. Wolfe)

## THE RPG VERSUS TANKS

Tanks and other AFVs are of course the primary target for RPGs and they have enjoyed much success in their intended role. An RPG warhead may not be able to defeat the frontal armor or gun mantlet of heavier tanks, but RPG fire can be effective against the sides and rear if enough rounds are fired (although modern composite armor such as Chobham usually defeats normal HEAT warheads). Most light AFVs such as armored personnel carriers (APCs), reconnaissance vehicles, or armored cars are generally easily defeated, although some modern vehicles such as the M2 Bradley infantry fighting vehicle and others fitted with additional special armor (ceramic appliqué armor, slat-armor and/or ERA) are more difficult to knock out. The media are quick to criticize any new AFV for lacking sufficient armor to defeat RPGs and similar weapons, seemingly amazed that a projectile costing less than $100 can destroy a vehicle costing millions. In fact, no AFV can carry the necessary 355mm of armor, even on just the front part, much less all around.

Even if the hull armor is penetrated, it often requires 4–6 rounds to ensure the vehicle is effectively knocked out. This is achieved by hitting the engine, igniting the fuel, detonating ammunition, or disabling the crew. When the HEAT round pierces the hull the penetrating slug, jet-like blast, and spalled fragments travel through the vehicle on a narrow path. Crewmen and equipment within its path are destroyed, but anything outside the path suffers little. In a lightly armored AFV, such as an APC, the slug may pass completely through. AFVs receiving multiple hits and casualties among the crew have continued to operate or at least disengage under their own power. It also requires multiple hits in the running gear to disable an AFV, breaking the track, knocking off road wheels, or shredding tires.

A former Soviet lieutenant reports the first RPG-7 demonstration firing he viewed as a cadet:

Before firing at the tank, we filled it with several sacks of earth. We were made to move away from the commander and plug our ears with cotton. The commander fired, a deafening explosion followed (our ears rang for days), and the grenade ploughed into the tank's turret. A while later, we removed remains of the earth from inside the tank and saw it had been turned into brick-like hot clumps, even though the grenade had penetrated only a few millimeters into the turret.

As we were told later, this surprising amount of damage was caused by the way the grenade was designed to concentrate the energy of the explosive and direct it in an immensely high-pressure stream that crushed the armor and destroyed everything inside the tank.

RPG users have learned that the most effective tactic against AFVs, besides attacking the sides and rear, is to fire large numbers of rounds from short ranges (to ensure good hits), from different directions, as rapidly as possible. There have been recorded attacks on single AFVs with 50 and more rounds fired. Typically, half-a-dozen good hits are required to knock a vehicle out. However, unless a fire is caused and ammunition detonated, a battle-damaged AFV can often be restored.

The most effective means of employing RPGs against tanks is to barrage-fire them in large numbers, with at least three weapons firing multiple rounds at the sides and back of the hull and into the running gear. Lighter AFVs may be engaged from any quadrant, but multiple hits are often still required.

Of course, AFVs are not the only targets. Soft-skin vehicles such as trucks, utility vehicles, automobiles, and vans are particularly vulnerable to RPGs and are common targets in an insurgency. Water craft from sampans to river patrol boats to barges have been targets as well. A HEAT round impacting the water throws up a narrow, 6m-high column of water. Iran's Islamic Revolutionary Guard Corps mounts RPG-7s on speedboats and they have fired on tankers and other large vessels. However, this is merely a harassing tactic as the RPG cannot inflict meaningful damage on large ships.

## THE "FLAK" RPG

One of the most unforeseen uses and successes of the RPG-7 is as an antiaircraft weapon. It was first used in this role in Vietnam, where it was preceded by the RPG-2. A significant number of helicopters have been downed by RPGs, with a major impact on some operations.

Helicopters carry virtually no armor; even attack helicopters carry little and certainly nothing that can protect against HEAT rounds. Engines, transmissions, drivetrains, control cables, hydraulics, fuel tanks, rotors, and nearly everything else is vulnerable. In a world where radar-directed antiaircraft guns and missiles or heat-seeking rockets were viewed as necessary to down aircraft, the RPG came as a shock.

Marines at Khe Sanh Combat Base duck for cover from mortar fire as a CH-46 helicopter makes its approach. It was when helicopters slowed and descended to land that they were especially vulnerable to RPG fire. (© Bettmann/Corbis)

Regardless of the furor over man-portable, shoulder-fired, heat-seeking surface-to-air missiles such as the Stinger, SA-7, and SA-14, there have been far, far more helicopters shot down by RPG-7s the world over – although the media frequently confuses RPGs with the various shoulder-fired, heat-seeking SAMs.

It was the VC and NVA who learned through trial and error how to engage helicopters with RPGs. Ideally they would fire them at helicopters when they transitioned from horizontal flight to a hover when landing, when on the ground, or when lifting off. They were static or moving very slowly and could not immediately evade. The gunners would fire immediately in front of a helicopter taking off. When ambushing landing zones they would ideally use three or more RPGs within 100m. They did not hesitate to fire on helicopters at low altitude in forward flight. Several decades later this practice was continued when one Black Hawk helicopter was downed by an RPG-7 in Iraq at a few hundred feet and at 150–200 knots. Being 32km from its base it was clearly not hit while landing or taking off.

On some occasions the range was just right and rounds self-destructed at their normal 920m. It was seldom that this could be done intentionally, owing to difficulties determining the exact range, angle of attack, and flight time. But there were instances in which the enemy conducted helicopter ambushes with multiple RPGs on approach routes into Free World bases.

Free World forces suffered hundreds of helicopters damaged or destroyed by RPGs in Vietnam and there was little that could be done about it. There were occasional incidents of RPG fire directed against helicopters around the world over the intervening years, but it was not until 1993 in the Horn of Africa that the world realized just how much impact the RPG-7 could have when engaging helicopters. The May 1993 battle of Mogadishu saw two US Black Hawk helicopters downed by RPG-7s, resulting in a major urban conflict during which three further helicopters were destroyed by RPGs.

The RPG-7 again raised its muzzle in Afghanistan and Iraq in the 21st century. Of the eight US helicopters lost to enemy action in Afghanistan between 2001 and 2009, seven were to RPGs; five of these were CH/MH-47 Chinooks, and numerous casualties resulted. In Iraq between 2003 and 2009 only six out of 40 US helicopters downed by enemy fire were reported hit by RPGs; however, it is possible that RPGs scored at least twice as highly, as many were listed only as "ground fire" or "undetermined."

The RPG has its limitations when employed against helicopters, including the difficulties of estimating range, angle of attack, and the lead necessary to hit a moving helicopter. Successful attacks, unless at close range on a hovering helicopter, are more of a matter of luck. Regardless, there is no doubt that the RPG will continue to be employed against helicopters and some efforts are being made to enhance their protection.

## THE RPG AS A BUNKER-BUSTER

Because of the nature of conflicts since the introduction of the RPG it is just as essential to engage field fortifications, defended buildings, and other structures as it is to attack AFVs. While a HEAT round will penetrate a considerable thickness of concrete, masonry, logs, sandbags, and packed earth, its terminal effect inside the structure is often disappointing. The blast jet is narrow and impacts into the opposite wall. It does not create a massive explosion (or fireball as depicted in movies) or blow structures apart. The projectile strikes the structure and detonates with a small flash generating some smoke and dust. There is some degree of overpressure and fragmentation inside the structure, but it may not wipe out or even wound all the occupants.

A HEAT projectile firing through a window will detonate when it strikes the opposite wall, causing more blast and fragmentation inside the room. Much of the blast will penetrate this wall into other rooms.

A Hamas militant fires an RPG-7 in Gaza City. Note the man to the right protecting his ears. The noise signature of an RPG is very high, making it uncomfortable to fire without ear protection. Firing without protection quickly results in permanent hearing damage. (© Mohammed Saber/epa/Corbis)

Window panes, blinds, and other window coverings may or may not detonate the projectile. The author once fired two RPG rounds at a *hooch* (bamboo hut) in an abandoned village in Vietnam to see the effects. The first round went through both sides and detonated in the trees beyond. The second detonated on contact, simply making a hole not much larger than the warhead and an even smaller hole in the opposite wall. If it had been occupied there would have been few casualties.

However, field fortifications made of rock known as sangars are particularly dangerous for the occupants as an RPG hit will blow even large rocks about and rock fragments are just as deadly as shrapnel. It helps to line the interior with sandbags.

### Helicopter ambush, Vietnam (previous pages)

The Viet Cong were quick to recognize the danger of helicopters. Free World forces could be inserted with little warning anywhere at any time. They allowed the infantry they carried to by-pass difficult terrain and other VC forces to attack at will in any direction. In areas where clearings suitable for helicopter landing zones were scarce the VC often established an ambush force armed with machine guns and a light portable weapon such as the RPG, which proved to be devastating to landing and departing helicopters. Here three VC, armed left to right, with a North Vietnamese-made B40, Chinese-made Type 56 (RPG-2), and Soviet RPG-7 engage UH-1H Huey helicopters on a hot landing zone. In actuality the launchers would have been spread out more and interspaced with machine gunners and riflemen. The leftmost B40 gunner is firing just ahead of a bird as it desperately takes off. In the middle the Type 56 gunner fires on an off-loading chopper. Even if he fails to hit the aircraft, he hopes to take out off-loading infantrymen. The RPG-7 gunner to the right fires on an inbound "slick," aiming well in front of it at maximum range in the hope of achieving an airburst when the round self-destructs.

Since the 1990s purpose-made rounds with thermobaric (TB) warheads have been developed specifically to defeat bunkers. These include the Russian TBG-7, Bulgarian GTB-7G, and Chinese WPF 2004. These 105mm warheads contain "slow-burning" explosive slurry, maintaining a longer detonation impulse. The mist-like slurry cloud penetrates into even small crevices as it detonates, creating a vacuum. This results in an implosion as air instantaneously blasts back into the vacuum, crushing everything in the immediate vicinity. It also causes concussion overpressure injuries and damage. Such a round blasts a hole through concrete and masonry, blows apart timber, sandbag, and earth bunkers, and can rip a 250mm hole through light armor. It is effective against personnel enclosed in structures under 300m$^3$, within 2m of an open position or trench, or within an 8m radius against personnel in the open.

## THE RPG AS AN ANTIPERSONNEL WEAPON

Shaped-charge warheads are far from ideal for antipersonnel use, but nonetheless RPGs are more often used against personnel than against any other target. The ideal personnel target is a small group. Much of the blast will be directed into the ground by the shaped-charge, but there will be significant surface blast and fragmentation. The fragments are mostly light and of irregular size as they are mainly bits of the warhead's sheet metal body. Nonetheless they are deadly. In Vietnam the author's company lost a man hit by a 1cm diameter bit of sheet metal in the heart. Secondary fragmentation is also a hazard in the form of gravel, rock fragments, and wood splinters.

The main deficiency of the RPG as an antipersonnel weapon is that most types of round lack a graze-fire capability. That is, when the projectile is traveling near horizontally and then impacts into the ground it often fails to detonate, as it needs to strike a near-vertical surface. The round may bury itself as an armed dud, ricochet and still end up as a dud, or break up. Rounds may pre-detonate when striking brush, twigs, vines, or similar objects.

In Vietnam RPGs would be barrage-fired – the most effective way to employ them against personnel – so that they would drop down through the trees, detonating on impact with the branches. The rounds would thus air-burst, blowing blast, fragmentation, and large splinters down onto troops below. This was done in an indirect fire manner from 300m or more. Extreme caution had to be used when firing at a high angle, as back blast deflected off the ground caused burn and debris injuries to the backs of legs. This was even more of a risk when firing on helicopters. An excited individual could easily become incautious and fire at a high angle, injuring himself. In fact insurgents have been identified owing to such injuries on the backs of their legs. In Afghanistan RPG-7s have been found with small steel plates welded to the bottom rim of the blast deflector to direct the blast slightly upward for firing at aircraft.

In urban and other close combat the short effective range of the RPG is not a hindrance, as ranges are seldom over 100m. Although not optimized for antipersonnel or antibuilding use, RPGs are more effective against personnel in buildings than small arms.

Despite the extent to which RPGs have been used against personnel, very few antipersonnel – that is, HE/frag – rounds have been developed and these are not often seen in the field. The available HE/frag rounds include the OG-7, OG-7M with a slightly longer range, OG-7G with a 60mm warhead (the others are 40mm), OG-7E with strictly a blast charge and light fragmentation, and rocket-assisted OFG-7 with a 270m direct fire range (the others reach around 150m and are not rocket-assisted, but propelled by the launcher charge only). Produced by Russia and Bulgaria, these rounds use the O-4M impact fuze as on 82mm mortar rounds.

Iran produced HE rounds by machining adapters to allow an 82mm mortar round without fins to be attached to a standard PG-7 tailboom. In 1990 Farabundo Marti National Liberation Front (FMLN) guerrillas in El Salvador produced a similar adaptation using Soviet 82mm and US 81mm M374 mortar shells. These heavy rounds had an estimated 150m range.

The author prepares to fire an RPG-2, 1969. Note the cotton in his ears and the Cambodian strikers in the background with hands over their ears. Like the RPG-7, the RPG-2 resounded with an ear-splitting crack.

## RPG ALLOCATION

In conventional armies using the RPG the most common allocation was simply one per rifle squad, be it motorized rifle, foot-mobile infantry, or paratroop. There are occasionally units with two per squad. They are manned by a gunner and an assistant (loader). The loader carries an assault rifle like other riflemen, and the gunner also often does. In some cases the gunner carries a pistol or compact personal defense weapon (Soviet 9mm APS Stechkin and Czechoslovak 7.65mm vz.61 Škorpion machine pistols). The Iraqis concentrated their RPG-7s in the company weapons platoon, which had 12 for attachment to rifle platoons. RPGs are also allocated to headquarters, service, support, engineer, and reconnaissance units for close-range antitank defense. The crew of each artillery piece, antiaircraft gun, and missile system has an RPG. In these cases, while individuals were trained to man the RPGs, they were not dedicated crewmen, but operated them as an additional duty.

RPG allocation in insurgent units is a different matter. Their small unit structure seldom follows a "table of organization," but is flexible and evolving. They will reallocate RPGs between subunits as necessary. Often small subunits, teams, groups, or squads (by whatever name they may be called) may have two or three RPGs, enabling them to concentrate their fire on enemy infantry, AFVs, or convoys by keeping up a high rate of fire. Some guerrilla bands concentrate all of their RPGs into a group for massed fire. There were instances in Afghanistan during the Soviet–Afghan War when 50 percent of a small unit was armed with RPGs.

## FIRING THE RPG-2

RPG-2 gunner training is very easy. The main challenges are range estimation, determining lead distances for moving targets, and allowing for crosswinds.

To load the launcher the hammer must be in the cocked position and the safety on. The hammer rebounds with the previous round. It is cocked by pushing down on a thumb lever on the rear of the trigger grip. The safety is placed in the armed position by pushing a stud on the left side of the trigger grip. To arm it the stud on the right side of the trigger grip is pressed. The safety is simply a push-through bar that blocks the cocked hammer. It will not fire in the armed position if the hammer is accidentally struck as a rebound-type hammer is used. A black powder propellant cartridge is screwed on to the end of the projectile's tailboom and inserted in the launcher's muzzle. The six folding tailfins are warped around the tailboom and spring open upon leaving the muzzle. A small stamped stud is found at the connection of the warhead and tailboom. This is aligned with a notch in the top of the tube's muzzle. The keyed alignment ensures that the ignition primer is aligned over the firing pin.

The launcher must be fired from only the right shoulder as a small gas escape port is located on the right side of the trigger grip. Hands must be kept clear of this vent. The launcher is placed on the right shoulder with the right hand on the trigger grip and the left hand (knuckles to the right, thumb forward) gripping the heat guard just behind the rear sight. The estimated range is selected on the graduated rear sight. From top to bottom the rear sight is graduated at 150, 100, and 50m. The safety stud is pressed to arm the launcher and the trigger squeezed. Firing is accompanied by a loud crack (hearing protection is essential) and a large cloud of white smoke to the rear and a smaller horizontal plume to the front. When the author fired an RPG-2 the first time without protection it felt as if nails were driven into both ears. At night there is a significant back blast flash and slight muzzle flash. A firing position must be selected that offers at least 1m clear of any form of obstructions to the rear, preferably more. The back blast safety area requires 25m clear of personnel, munitions, equipment, and flammable materials.

## FIRING THE RPG-7

Plastic-wrapped RPG-7 rounds are packed six to a wooden case along with propellant charges held in plastic tubes. The plastic wrap is removed when the projectiles are placed in the carrier, but the propellant charges are kept in their tubes.

If the iron sights are to be used both are raised. If the optical sight is used it is removed from its carrying case, snapped to the mount, and the forward sight cover removed. The launcher's bore is inspected, as is the projectile and the propellant charge.

The weapon is placed on safe by pushing the stud on the left side of the trigger grip and immediately behind the trigger. The safety is simply a push-through bar that blocks the hammer. Like the RPG-2, the RPG-7 will not fire in the armed position if the hammer is accidentally struck, as the hammer is of the rebound type.

The muzzle and breech covers are removed, after which the plastic shipping cap is unscrewed from the end of the projectile tailboom and the propellant charge screwed on. The projectile is slid into the muzzle. If a tight fit (propellant tubes can swell slightly) it needs to be twisted in counterclockwise (facing the direction of fire). Near the base of the warhead is a short round alignment pin that fits into a U-shaped notch in the top of the muzzle. This aligns the primer with the firing pin in the bottom of the barrel.

The fabric warning tag on the projectile's nose is pulled out with the two-prong retaining pin and the nose cap removed. In heavy rain, sleet, or hail the cap is left on to prevent premature detonation – however the arming pin is still removed.

The back blast danger area is 20m deep and 15m wide with another 25m-wide caution area. A firing position must be selected that offers at least 2m clear of any form of obstructions to the front and rear and the muzzle must have at least 200mm of clearance from surrounding obstructions to allow the folding fins to deploy. It requires at least a 1sq m opening (door or window) to the rear or side to prevent excessive blast overpressure. If firing from a fighting position, trench, or ditch the breech must be clear of the position's back wall and parapet to avoid severe blast reflection. When firing from the prone position the legs must be angled 45 degrees to the left to keep them clear of the back blast.

The launcher is placed on the right shoulder; the trigger grip is held by the right hand and the rear pistol grip with the left. Hand positions can be reversed. Some operators hold the trigger grip with the right hand and place the left over the tube, pressing it on to the shoulder.

The launcher is pointed downrange, the hammer on the back of the grip is cocked by pushing it downward with the thumb, the weapon is taken off safe by pressing the button on the right side of the trigger grip, and the finger is placed on the trigger.

The range is determined on the optical sight's range scale and, for a moving target, the lead determined. If the iron sights are being used the range is estimated on the graduated rear sight. From top to bottom the rear sight is graduated at 500, 400, 300, and 200m. These ranges are designated on the sight by 5, 4, 3, and 2. The optical sight's reticle is graduated for range in the same manner. If the air temperature is above 0°C (32°F) the optical sight's temperature compensation knob is set on [+]. If it is below freezing it is set on [-].

The weapon is sighted and the trigger squeezed. The firing report is a piercingly loud crack and, as with the RPG-2, ear protection is essential. Concussion from muzzle and back blast is inconsequential unless firing from within a structure or open field fortification, or from the prone position in which cases there is some blast reflection. Absolutely no recoil is felt, just the immediate absence of the projectile's weight.

There is a fireball and bluish-white smoke puff 0.9–1.2m in diameter to the rear, which may linger up to eight seconds in light winds, but usually dissipates rapidly. Depending on soil conditions there may be considerable dust (or kicked-up snow or rain-spray) raised when firing from the prone or kneeling position. The muzzle flash is small and the rocket charge will ignite about 11m in front of the muzzle, creating a small puff of smoke. The rocket ignition is virtually simultaneous with the launch. The projectile will impact on a 150m-range target in about a half-second. The author's experience with firing at targets within 50–70m was that the projectile impact was almost simultaneous with firing. Sometimes the tailboom or the base of the warhead was blown back a short distance roughly toward the firer.

A tracer is fitted into the tailboom to allow the gunner to follow its flight and more effectively and quickly correct his aim for a follow-on shot in the event of a miss. An experienced gunner tracking the tracer can sense a miss before the projectile even passes the target and will prepare to fire a second round. It requires approximately 14 seconds to

reload, acquire a target, and sight it; if firing in barrages at a larger target or area target the weapon can be fired in 9 or 10 seconds. The detonation is a relatively small burst of dark gray smoke and dust.

Much is made of the fact that the firing signature reveals the firing position. That is a consideration in some circumstances, but typically in close-range combat there are so many weapons firing from different directions and ranges with so much incoming and outgoing fire, smoke and dust, and confusion that it is very difficult to locate RPG firing positions. It is even more difficult in urban areas, forests, jungles, rocky hills, or mountains. Gunners are trained to relocate immediately after firing. Insurgents in particular have learned to select positions in unlikely areas with covered escape routes; they use the smoke and dust as a screen and move out immediately, rapidly setting up alternative positions to keep up a high rate of fire.

Gunner proficiency does not require a great deal of training. A man able to fire a rifle has no trouble with an RPG. Firing three to six rounds will make any combatant proficient enough for targets at 150m or less. After firing two or three dozen rounds a gunner will be able to engage targets at 300m, perhaps 500m. As a result, RPGs are a good investment, and gaining proficiency is cheap. In places like Afghanistan rounds go for as little as US $10. This low cost, easy of use and obvious combat effectiveness mean that few weapons can compete with the RPG.

A Mahdi Army militiaman sights an RPG-7 in Basra, 2008. It is loaded with an HE/frag round. Firing from the left shoulder is awkward and sighting is difficult. (Essam Al-Sudani/AFP/Getty Images)

## Engaging the Enemy

When a rocket deviates only slightly from a target in range, the adjustment of fire is accompanied by shifting the aimpoint in height. If a rocket falls short of the target, raise the aimpoint upwards on the profile of the target (aim at the upper edge), and if the rocket flies over the target, aim lower by half a silhouette (aim at the lower edge of the target).

If the range error is great, it is necessary to determine the magnitude of deviation in meters and correspondingly select a new marking on the sight scale (setting on the mechanical sight).

If a rocket misses the target both in range and windage, then the adjustment for range and windage is made simultaneously. When adjusting fire during the engagement of moving targets, it is necessary to take into account whether the target is approaching (or going away) during the time expended in preparation for the subsequent shot.

The RPG-7's muzzle velocity is 117m/s (384fps). Approximately 11m into its flight the rocket ignites to propel the warhead to 294m/s (965fps). The PG-7 warhead self-destructs approximately 920m from the launcher. (Artwork by Peter Bull Art Studio)

**First shot – miss:**

This view through the reticle of an RPG-7 shows the rocket detonation offset from the target.

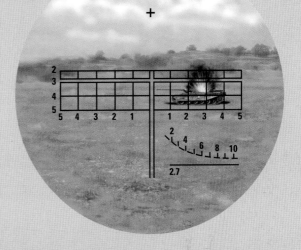

**Follow-up shot:**

This second view shows the RPG-7 gunner successfully hitting the target by aiming lower and to the right of the target.

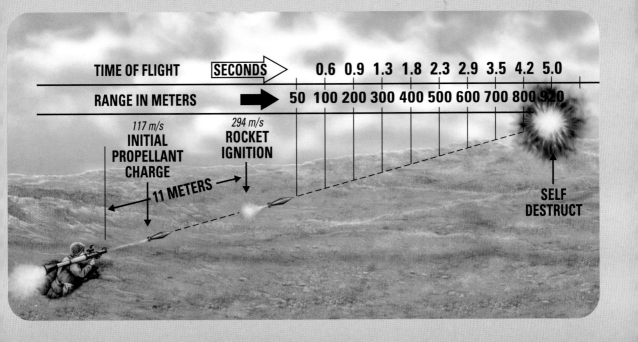

TIME OF FLIGHT ⟩SECONDS⟩ 0.6 0.9 1.3 1.8 2.3 2.9 3.5 4.2 5.0

RANGE IN METERS ➡ 50 100 200 300 400 500 600 700 800 920

117 m/s
INITIAL PROPELLANT CHARGE

294 m/s
ROCKET IGNITION

← 11 METERS →

SELF DESTRUCT

# RPG EMPLOYMENT TECHNIQUES

## The original Soviet concept

The basic Soviet concept of RPG-7 use was straightforward, with rewards which far outweighed the initial costs. The RPG was viewed as a unit's final antitank defense within the overall antitank defense plan. This plan was referred to as a "zone of continuous antitank fire" and involved all available antitank weapons. Warsaw Pact armies as well as client states employed the same tactics, but of course much adapted to their own equipment limitations, terrain, and climate, as well as tactical considerations that took into account the circumstances of their enemies.

According to this overall plan, artillery would engage approaching armor formations at long range. Wire-guided antitank missiles, both man-portable and AFV-mounted, would engage at the maximum range possible – theoretically 3,000m, but terrain and vegetation masking usually shortened this, while evasive maneuvers, smoke, dust, and counterfire also hampered such long-range engagements. Tank guns would next open up at ranges of over 1,000m followed by battalion-level 73mm SPG-9 recoilless guns and 73mm guns on BMP infantry fighting vehicles at ranges under 1,000m. All of these weapons would continue to fire on enemy AFVs, and the last layer of defense was the RPG-7, preferably in an ambush. With nine RPG-7s on a company frontage several hundred meters wide the close-range antitank fires would be dense. These would be backed by RPG-18 single-shot rocket launchers, three or four per squad, and then RKG-3 antitank hand grenades as an absolute last-ditch defense. A company might position one or more RPG teams forward of the main position, especially in trees and heavy brush, to ambush approaching AFVs from the flanks and rear.

In the defense RPG-7 positions were normally selected in the center of the squad sector, but they could be emplaced anywhere to best cover AFV approaches and gaps between adjacent units. They would ideally be placed in depth through the unit position with some assigned to protect flanks and gaps. Alternative firing positions were prepared if time permitted. RPG-7s assigned to headquarters and support units would add to the depth of the defense.

In the attack, although the Soviets relied primarily on the tank and the weapons aboard BMPs for antitank firepower, RPG-7s also had their uses. Infantrymen could dismount from their APCs and engage AFVs and fire on enemy positions and defended buildings; or they could fire from APC open-top hatches. Another Soviet offensive tactic for RPGs was reconnaissance-in-force, essentially a raid, to attack enemy positions and destroy static AFVs and other weapon systems at close range as well as grab prisoners. When fighting dismounted the RPG gunner was in the center of the squad line next to the squad leader for close control, with the assistant to the gunner's left. But Soviet soldiers also reported another use. Being forbidden to fraternize with locals while on maneuvers in East Germany, they could watch girls from afar through the optical sight.

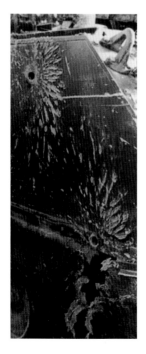

These may be 57mm recoilless rifle or RPG-7 hits on the engine compartment of an M113A1 APC in Vietnam, probably the former. However the results and appearance are much the same.

58

# Vietnam

The RPG-2 and Type 56 saw use from early on in Vietnam. These proved to be effective against the light armor employed by the South Vietnamese: M24 light tanks, M113 APCs, and V-100 armored cars. At the beginning of 1965 the M24s began to be replaced by M41A3 light tanks, but they fared little better against RPGs. The Vietnamese would fasten sand-filled ammunition cans to the front and sides of tank turrets to detonate RPG and recoilless rifle rounds. The first US M48A3 tanks arrived with the Marines in July 1965 and with the Army the following March. The RPG-2 had little effect on the front quadrant of the heavy tanks. However, the M113, which was in wide use, and the Marine AAV-7 amphibious assault vehicles and Ontos M50A1 antitank vehicles were all vulnerable to RPGs – so much so that troops preferred to ride atop the vehicles rather than suffer a troop compartment hit. The M113A1 with its aluminum armor was especially vulnerable if penetrated: if an internal fire ignited it melted and the vehicle was a total loss. RPGs were also directed against riverine craft, patrol boats, and helicopters.

However, a study showed that statistically, only one out of every eight to ten rounds typically struck the targeted APC. Due to the extreme angles of warhead impact, the penetrating blast effect was also often dispersed, and thus only one out of every seven hits actually penetrated the hull, with an average of only 0.8 casualties per penetration. Tanks with sloped armor fared even better.

But the following description of the damage inflicted on all three types of tracked vehicles in the Marine inventory by RPG-7s during an ambush in July 1967 provides an insight into the weapon's effectiveness when sufficient rounds could be fired:

> Tracked vehicles suffered all along the column. An RPG round penetrated both sides of an LVTE1 [landing vehicle, tracked, engineer, Mk I] moving with Company E. Another RPG explosion disabled the turret of a [M48A3] tank with Company F, wounding three crewmen. When Company H brought up an Ontos to suppress NVA fire that was holding up its movement, an RPG gunner hit the vehicle and wounded [the] three crewmen. A second Ontos came forward, beat down the enemy fire with its machine gun, and permitted the company to move again.

RPG-2s and 7s were excellent fire-support weapons for NVA assaults, fired rapidly and directed mainly at perimeter bunkers.

The RPG-7 began to be fielded in late 1967 and as a result the NVA passed their RPG-2s to the VC. The upgraded equipment was an instant success for both the NVA and VC. Recoilless rifles had been available to the VC prior to this, but they were extremely heavy to man-pack through jungles, swamps, and hills. The RPG was much more portable and packed a powerful punch for such a light weapon. In addition, the NVA's newly received RPG-7 could penetrate the rear quadrant of the M48 Patton. To counteract this, the US soldiers fastened their sand-filled 20mm and 40mm ammunition cans together with water cans on the turret rear, while spare track links were hung on the turret front. Tank gunners were directed to be prepared to fire coaxial and turret-top machine guns and main gun flechette rounds at short ranges to tackle any approaching RPG gunners. There were instances when the NVA used RPGs equipped with night vision sights to ambush armor patrols.

Achieving successful hits against an M48 required optimum conditions, however. In one instance during the 1968 Tet Offensive, an M48A3 remained operational after 19 RPG hits at Bien Hoa Air Base, again with the extreme angles of impact saving the vehicle. When M551 Sheridan light tanks were introduced in 1969 they proved vulnerable to RPGs; during the first three months of service of the first 60 deployed, an armored cavalry squadron commander described the RPG attacks as often devastating to the Sheridans. Nevertheless, the assessment team accompanying the initial deployment determined that the M551s provided better protection from RPGs and mines than the aluminum-armored M113 APCs.

One Vietnam veteran observed:

> It matters little in these conditions that it [RPG-7] gives the shooter's position away. Let me tell you from personal experience, as the target of the weapon on at least 14 occasions, I don't ever recall "pinpointing" the position from which the projectile was launched. I might have seen it from the corner of my eye, and then focused fire in that general or immediate vicinity ... but the dust, chaos and excitement of such combat makes us far less effective than we are on the range ... and this is particularly true when the weapon scores a direct hit. The concussion is incredible, and the shrapnel is very effective, stunning the victims to a point of being completely disabled for several seconds if not minutes, depending on the severity of the hit. The jet of flame in the HEAT round is extraordinarily long. I took a hit in the left rear corner of my M113A1 ACAV[1] at about two-thirds up from the lower edge of the side (fuel tank side, by the way ... we were diesel and luckily did not ignite from this hit though it did hole the fuel tank), and the flame actually cut through the rear ramp exit door slicing it as if it had been cut with a torch. This slice was well over 18in [45.7cm] long. If you happen to be unlucky enough to be standing in the path of this lightning bolt when it hits the side of the armor, you can well imagine the carnage.

[1] Armored Cavalry Assault Vehicle, an up-gunned M113A1 APC.

In the Ben Cui Rubber Plantation in September 1968 the NVA launched four assaults in nine days against a mechanized infantry battalion, using small arms, machine guns, mortars, and RPGs. The only real damage during those nine days was caused by the RPGs. The battalion adopted a standard kit with a 15.25m-long, 2.5m-high section of chain-link fence and barbed wire pickets for each AFV. Crews erected the screen some 2.5m forward of their vehicle (see the Impact chapter for a detailed discussion of RPG screens). Following the engagements, battalion vehicles were not considered combat-ready unless they had the RPG screen. Once the battalion adopted RPG screens crews would repeatedly find RPG tailbooms hanging in their fences following engagements. The battalion's losses to RPGs dropped drastically after the screens were introduced.

The real value of the RPG to the NVA/VC was as a close-range fire support weapon. They did not let the lack of HE/frag warheads deter them. When attacking firebases and other installations the RPG teams would move in close to the base on either side of the attack lane. When the attack was launched the RPGs were fired at the perimeter bunkers and other positions. At longer ranges they would simply barrage-fire rounds into the base with no attempt to hit specific targets. Sappers infiltrating through barrier wire would often carry RPGs to attack bunkers, gun positions, command posts, and parked aircraft once inside the base. In vehicle ambushes they seldom engaged at over 50–75m, where one out of three rounds hit the targets. They might have used two to four RPGs to initiate the ambush and held one or two in reserve to engage other targets.

RPGs were also used against personnel in ambushes, longer-range direct fire, and even rudimentary indirect fire from several hundred meters, usually resulting in tree bursts. The author's Cambodian strike force company sometimes carried captured RPG-2s for counterfire; although American units in the area had to be informed of their presence to prevent them calling in artillery on their firing signature.

Lebanon, 2004. A Fatah militia leader is accompanied by a young Palestinian boy, a member of the Martyrs of Jenin, who is holding an RPG-7 – illustrating how extremely young children frequently receive weapons indoctrination in some wartorn areas. (Ramzi Haidar/AFP/Getty Images)

During the 1973 Yom Kippur War Syrian RPG-7 teams infiltrated through porous Israeli lines on the Golan Heights to launch close-range surprise attacks on Israeli armor. These Syrian troops are dug in on a hillside facing the Israeli positions.

## The Middle East

The first combat use of the RPG-7 was by Egypt during the 1967 Six-Day War. Only one was assigned per platoon, backed by RPG-43 antitank grenades. They were found to be highly effective and impressed the Israelis; the Israel Defense Forces (IDF) captured enough to issue them to paratroop and commando battalions. However, even though they had been exposed to the RPG-7 both as a target and as a user, the Israelis were still taken by surprise by the destructive power of the RPG-7 during the 1973 Yom Kippur War. Five Egyptian infantry divisions successfully crossed the Suez Canal without any armor support, which would not arrive until a full 12 hours later. They were reinforced with numerous man-portable AT-3 Sagger wire-guided missiles and RPG-7s. Until this armor support arrived, Egyptian penetration into the Sinai Peninsula was limited as they were forced to remain within the air defense missile umbrella arrayed on the Canal's west side. But this in turn limited Israeli close air support to the counterattacking armored brigades.

In advance of the Israeli attack Egyptian infantry carried the AT-3s and spare RPG rounds forward to the front line of defenses in two-wheel carts. When the attack was launched an Israeli tank commander reported seeing Egyptian soldiers rushing forward in pairs 150–200m beyond their positions before disappearing from their line of sight. As the Israeli tanks rolled forward they began receiving artillery fire and, as they emerged from the dust, barrages of AT-3 missiles streaked at them with the tanks immediately taking hits as they closed in on the Egyptian positions. Scores of RPG-7 rounds were then fired from the flanks as tanks passed the hidden gunners. Evasive maneuvers were undertaken and in the resulting confusion, smoke, and dust the attack lost its momentum. Many units were forced to withdraw. The RPG-7 had undoubtedly proved its worth in its original antitank defensive role.

Syrian forces also employed the RPG-7 in large numbers during the Yom Kippur War and one claim is that they inflicted more losses on Israeli AFVs than any other weapon. As on the Suez Front, Israeli armor on the Golan Heights was without infantry and Syrian RPG teams infiltrated among the tanks, knocking out many.

In later Israeli–Palestinian conflicts the RPG-7, now employed in larger numbers, again influenced battles, and Israeli victories came at a high cost. One result was the addition of appliqué armor and ERA to many Israeli AFVs. They also fielded heavy APCs – that is, APCs built on obsolescent tank hulls – for added protection in close-in urban assaults. The Israelis, however, captured even more RPG-7s and ammunition and they were more widely issued.

In the more recent conflicts where the Palestinians possessed more modern ATGMs, the RPG-7 still claimed a considerable share of victims. They had little effect against Merkava tanks during the 2006 war against Hezbollah, but the Israelis were forced to withdraw their M113s due to the latter's light armor and vulnerability. RPGs have continued to be used in all post-1973 conflicts by Syrians, Lebanese, and the many Palestinian factions including by the Palestine Liberation Organization (PLO), Hamas, and Hezbollah. The PLO distributed one RPG-7 to every three to six fighters.

## Soviet–Afghan War

In Afghanistan in 1979–89, and again in Chechnya during the Chechen Wars of the 1990s, the Russians quickly learned just how effective the RPG-7 was when it was turned on them and used in unexpected ways. In Afghanistan the Soviets escorted tanks with dismounted infantry and following light AFVs, but barrages of six or more would nevertheless be fired at the tanks and escorts at ranges as close as 20–50m. Well-concealed positions were dug and occasionally areas 2–3m behind the position were doused with water as an ingenious way of preventing the gunners' positions from being exposed by the rising dust. The *mujahideen* found that RPGs were particularly effective when neutralizing infantry or knocking out escort vehicles. They also kept the infantry well away from the tanks as hits on or near the tanks caused numerous casualties. Once the escorts had been driven off, the *mujahideen* would close in from behind and barrage-fire at the tanks' rear while other groups kept the infantry away with machine guns.

The *mujahideen* often operated in 20–30-man groups and might have as many as 15–20 RPGs, although frequently fewer. This enabled them to fire barrages when mortars were not available, and the RPGs were certainly lighter than mortars and their ammunition. In dense brush areas the Soviets laid down a continuous barrage of HE/frag rounds ahead of them to destroy or drive away hidden RPG teams.

An Afghan *mujahideen* fighter rests during the 1989 attack on Jalalabad, Afghanistan. RPG-7s are just as effective when used in built-up areas to attack fortified buildings as they are against armored vehicles. (Photo by David Stewart-Smith/Getty Images)

The Afghans also employed RPG-7s against Soviet helicopters with some success, especially when they could ambush landing helicopters or catch them with barrages flying down narrow valleys. A head-on shot within 100m was particularly effective. It was the success of these attacks that spawned the idea of providing the *mujahideen* with US Stinger missiles, which eventually turned the war in their favor.

Of course, throughout the Soviet–Afghan War (and later in the Chechen Wars), the RPG was a vital component of the Soviets' own weapon arsenal. Recognizing the fire-support capabilities of the RPG, some Soviet units within Afghanistan added a second to their squads. In more open areas offering concealing gullies and rock outcroppings the Soviets fanned out infantry ahead of the AFVs to clear and outpost areas. The *Spetznaz* brigades deployed to Afghanistan were armed with RPG-16s and single-shot RPG-22s; however, both were poorly suited for antipersonnel and antifortification use, so instead they reequipped themselves with captured Type 69-Is and RPG-7s which were being supplied to the *mujahideen* by China and Pakistan. In 1980 the US had purchased and provided these RPG-7s to the *mujahideen*, each provided with 20 rounds. Inspired by their obvious success, in 1985 the CIA provided 10,000 more RPG-7s with 200,000 rounds, although it failed to provide further ammunition for the previously supplied RPG-7s.

## Chechnya

During the Chechen Wars of 1994–96 and 1999–2000, the Chechens also used large numbers of RPGs, but in an urban setting rather than barren mountains. As well as capturing many RPGs, they took over Soviet army bases and training centers. The exceedingly vicious battle for Grozny saw extensive use of RPG-7s and 18s in the close-quarters street fighting that halted most Russian armored columns. Here too RPGs were barrage-fired, sometimes in phenomenal numbers. It is claimed that in January and February 1995, the Russians lost over 100 tanks and 250 other AFVs in Grozny.

The Chechen rebel forces used tactics similar to those of the *mujahideen* that were even more effective among the urban rubble. They would have two or more alternative positions selected and each gunner would be accompanied by two or three AK-armed men carrying extra rounds, who would open up with suppressive fire as the gunner changed positions. They would also "hug" the Soviets, operating within 100m of Russian forces, which maximized their effectiveness and prevented artillery and air strikes from being called in.

Chechen fighters moving to new positions inside Grozny, January 1995. Two to three Kalashnikov-armed men escorted RPG gunners and each carried one or two extra RPG rounds. Sometimes they would carry them to the front and drop them off in forward stockpiles. (Pascal Guyot/AFP/Getty Images)

The Chechens fired RPGs at anything that moved. They were fired at high angles over low buildings and in unaimed volleys from between buildings. Controlled volley fire was also used. The Russians had not considered RPGs effective in the close confines of built-up areas, and nor of much use in roles other than antitank, despite the successes of Russian-backed forces in Vietnam. The T-90 tank, which the Russians touted as indestructible, was frequently knocked out by three or four RPG-7 hits during the height of the Chechen War. When the Soviets started fitting ERA on their tanks the rebels fired an RPG within 50m to detonate the bricks, after which two or more RPGs were fired at the exposed point. However this was only effective at these close ranges as the RPG is not precisely accurate, especially against a moving vehicle.

The Chechens employed 25-man "platoons" of three small "squads." Each squad had one or two RPG gunners with RPG-7s and/or 18s, two machine gunners, and a few riflemen/snipers. The RPGs were the core of their firepower. One squad would take ground floor window positions on one side of a street (none on the opposite side to avoid firing into one another). The other squads would be in basements down the street in the direction from which the Russian tanks entered the kill zone. The ambush squad would open fire, backed by snipers and grenadiers on upper floors and roofs, above the height range of tank guns, dropping bundles of antitank grenades. The lead and tail AFVs would be knocked out first to trap the others. The waiting squads then emerged and attacked the Russians from the rear, firing from basement windows at which the tanks could not depress their guns. RPGs would also engage tanks from building roofs to exploit thinner turret-top and engine deck armor.

There are claims that the Chechens placed more explosives in RPG rounds to achieve better penetration. However, this is technically impossible. There is no space for additional explosives behind the existing charge and it certainly cannot be placed in the hollow-charge cavity without losing the hollow-charge effect. They may have been able to place charges in the cavity and nosecone (although this is not designed to be opened), but this would completely unbalance the round, drastically affecting trajectory and range. Such tampered-with RPGs could be useful against personnel and buildings, but only at ranges under 30–40m.

## Other conflicts

The *mujahideen* learned much in regard to the employment of the RPG-7 during the 1979–89 Soviet–Afghan War, techniques which were passed on by Al-Qaeda operatives who had participated in the war to Somali rebels and Iraqi insurgents in later conflicts. In Iraq, because of the Iraqi insurgents' low level of training and the RPG's long-range inaccuracy they are most often fired in barrages from multiple launchers. This technique is usually used against helicopters, vehicles, and installations. Small unit engagements, especially patrols encircled by insurgents, will

Somali Islamist rebels in Mogadishu, Somalia with an RPG-7 loaded with a battered PG-7M HEAT round. It is not uncommon for rounds to be retained in stockpiles, hidden, carried about, and traded for lengthy periods before finally being used. Note the weapon lacks an optical sight. Over time many of these become lost or damaged through hard use. (© Ismail Warsameh/XinHua/Xinhua Press/Corbis)

also receive barrage fire, often from "long range" as the fighters close in with AK-47s and machine guns. A dozen to a score of RPGs have been massed against a single US tank and fired in barrages. One claim states that 50 were fired at a single tank.

RPGs have also been widely used in Africa's wars, beginning in the 1966–89 South African Border War and the 1964–79 Rhodesian Bush War, as well as numerous later civil wars. They appear to have been used more sparingly in the first two conflicts, but nonetheless made their mark where the primary targets were light AFVs.

Terrorists, narco-gangs, and other criminal groups worldwide have used RPGs to attack embassies, consulates, radio and television stations, government buildings, automobiles, buses, parked airliners, and anything else presenting a target. The RPG is a potent weapon and easily concealed, which allows it to be secreted into the desired firing area, giving the assailant the advantage of surprise in addition to effectiveness.

### Slaughter of the tanks, Grozny, Chechnya (Previous pages)

The Russians entered Grozny with no practical tactics for the situation they faced. There were no front lines or identifiable defended areas. The Chechen guerrillas would conduct hit-and-run attacks and ambushes on Russian incursions probing into the destroyed city. The Russians usually placed their T-90 tanks, often fitted with ERA, in the lead as they were better protected against RPGs. The more vulnerable BMP-1 APCs and other supporting AFVs were to the rear providing covering fire. Chechen attacks could come from any direction and usually from multiple directions. They would open fire, not all at once, but with a phased planning to knock out lead and rear AFVs, command vehicles, and intended to separate the dismounted infantry and supporting vehicles from the tanks. The Chechens engaged from basement windows, from the ground floors, upper floors, roofs, and street barricades. The RPG-7 was a key to the success of these tactics, as it was easily carried through the rubble, and offered a high rate of fire and deadly effectiveness against AFVs, buildings, and personnel. **1.** The lead T-90 is attacked by RPGs from the rear fired from above. **2.** The rear BMP is likewise engaged in an effort to block the other vehicles, even though the boulevard is broad. **3.** The second T-90 is hit with a barrage of RPGs fired from behind a barricade as the tank passes a side street. **4.** An RPG is fired from a roof to attack a BMP's thinner top armor. It also presents a larger target from this angle. **5.** Rifle and machine gun fire would then engage the dismounted infantry protecting the AFVs, who will also be fired on by RPGs.

# IMPACT
## "The best handheld antitank gun in the world"

The RPG has had a surprising impact on its opponents in conflicts in which it has been used in any significant numbers. This includes the Yom Kipper War, Vietnam, Somalia, Chechnya, Afghanistan (against both Soviet and NATO forces), and Iraq. US soldiers have been so impressed with the RPG that it has been proposed that it be copied and used by the US. One such proposal was made by General William Westmoreland, commander of the US forces in Vietnam, but this idea was rejected by the Ordnance Corps. The RPG-7 was finally tested by the US Army Ordnance Department at Aberdeen Proving Ground, Maryland, in 1969 and the early 1970s. The tests had two purposes: to ascertain its capabilities and limitations, and to determine if there was a requirement for a similar weapon for US forces. It was eventually decided that a similar weapon was not required as the M72-series LAW, 90mm recoilless rifle, and the yet-to-be-fielded Dragon wire-guided ATGM system fulfilled the requirements for small-unit antiarmor defense. Despite this, General Creighton Abrams, Westmoreland's successor, was equally convinced by the RPG, stating that "the B41/RPG-7 is the best handheld antitank gun in the world."

Indeed, its flexibility when used imaginatively and its light weight, compactness, and sheer numbers have made the RPG a deadly entity on the battlefield the world over. It is not often that a single weapon system has had such a major impact in a battle as the RPG-7.

The battle of Mogadishu of May 3–4, 1993 saw two MH-60 Black Hawk helicopters downed by RPG-7s during a failed Ranger raid. It resulted in a significant battle to extract the raiders and rescue crash survivors. Of the friendly casualties there were 18 dead and 83 wounded

A Somali Islamist fighter carrying an RPG-7 moves into position in strife-ridden Mogadishu during a 2009 action against African Union peacekeeping troops. (Mohamed Dahir /AFP/Getty Images)

Americans, one dead Malaysian, and two wounded Pakistanis. Besides the downed choppers, a number of these casualties were caused by RPGs on the ground; in addition an MH-6 Little Bird attack helicopter and two additional Black Hawks were damaged by RPGs, but made it to the airport before crash-landing. The impact of this battle led to widespread repercussions within the US Army and the government and even resulted in international policy changes. If it had not been for simple little RPGs knocking down two helicopters, the raid's outcome would have been very different.

The US armed forces have faced the RPG-7 in Vietnam, Grenada, Panama, the Gulf War, Somalia, various African contingency operations, Bosnia, Kosovo, Afghanistan, and Iraq, yet only lip service has been paid to its use. The US Army did provide a polyurethane and steel mock-up training aid of the RPG-7 and its projectile, designated DVC-T 30-5, in the 1970s and 1980s, but these are now generally unavailable. This was merely a device to be carried by Opposing Forces (OPFOR) soldiers as a visual signature and offered no means of replicating the RPG in force-on-force training exercises. On the whole, the US Army has done a poor job of replicating the RPG, its capabilities, and its varied and imaginative means of employment in training exercises. Now they are facing it yet again as one of the primary insurgent weapons in Iraq and Afghanistan.

During pre-mobilization training an Ohio National Guardsman clothed as an Iraqi insurgent fires a Viper Multiple Integrated Laser Engagement System (MILES) antiarmor rocket simulator, which is used to simulate RPG-7 firing signatures in exercises. The Viper is mainly used to replicate the M136 (AT4) LAW in force-on-force training exercises. (US Army/Spc Ryan A. Cleary)

## COMBATING THE EFFECTS OF THE RPG

In Vietnam in 1967 the US Army undertook a study of the effects of RPGs against bunkers and examined means of protecting them. It disseminated the results in a technical intelligence brief, *Protection of Friendly Bunkers from Effects of the RPG-2 and RPG-7 Antitank Launchers* (Tech Intel Brief 1-68) in 1968 and provided an accompanying 16mm film. The results of this study are described below (p. 74). In 1976 the Army produced *Soviet RPG-7 Antitank Grenade Launcher: Capabilities and Countermeasures* (TRADOC Bulletin 3[u]) and an accompanying videotape based on lessons learned from the 1973 Yom Kippur War. In 1980 it provided an RPG-7 operator's manual, but that was the extent of the effort invested. Given that the RPG-7 is still widely used throughout the world by armies, guerrillas and terrorists in all tactical environments, it is surprising that the US Army has not made a greater effort to depict the employment of the weapon in training exercises at the Combat Training Centers.[1] For years all recommendations to field an RPG-7 MILES[2] laser simulator were ignored because of the extra costs, and senior officers were under the misconception that the Viper MILES simulator could

[1] Joint Readiness Training Center, Louisiana; National Training Center, California; and Combat Maneuver Training Center, Germany.
[2] MILES is Multiple Integrated Laser Engagement System in which eye-safe laser transmitters are attached to weapons and receptors are fitted on troops and vehicles to indicate hits during force-on-force exercises. The Viper was to replicate the XM132 antiarmor rocket, the intended replacement for the M72A3 LAW. The Viper was a failure and the Swedish M136 (AT4) was adopted. The Viper simulator is used to replicate the AT4 and, inadequately, sometimes the RPG-7.

act as a substitute. These were only employed in small numbers and seldom was an effort made to replicate the tactics and techniques used by guerrillas. As a result, US forces were ill-prepared to face the RPG-7 in Afghanistan and Iraq. This has, however, been rectified to some degree at the Combat Training Centers as their focus has shifted to preparing units for deployment to Afghanistan and Iraq.

In 2006 Saab Training Systems of Sweden introduced an RPG-7 simulator providing OPFOR troops with a realistic replica fitted with a MILES system. When "fired" it projects an invisible eye-safe laser beam and also generates a flash and sound effect. The target AFV has laser receptors attached about the vehicle. When a hit is scored a "kill" light flashes, signaling that the vehicle is disabled. The reinforced polyurethane simulator is 1,200mm long, weighs 6.9kg, and is provided with a removable non-flight "projectile." The simulator is preset with a delay before it can be fired again to replicate reload time. The total number of rounds fired can be set to limit it to the crew's basic load. It is hoped that increased exposure to this will result in better responses to RPG fire on the battlefield.

## Protecting AFVs against RPGs

Armor thick enough to resist RPGs or any HEAT round cannot be fitted on light AFVs, soft-skin vehicles, and watercraft. Alternatives are not completely effective, but do provide some degree of protection.

In 1966 "bar-armor" was fitted to various river assault craft in Vietnam. It comprised of a system of 75mm spaced horizontal 16mm-diameter steel bars attached to mounting brackets on the sides of hulls and superstructures. The space between the bars and deckhouse would often be used to stow C-ration cases, which defeated the bar-armor's standoff effect. RPG warheads striking one of the bars detonated a sufficient distance, 30–45cm, from the hull/superstructure to prevent penetration. A warhead striking between two bars would short out its piezoelectric detonating system and break up without exploding.

A similar form of RPG armor working on the same principle is the "slat-armor" cage or "birdcage armor" fitted to all Stryker combat vehicles in Iraq and Afghanistan. This is a frame of horizontal bars appearing like open Venetian blinds fitted to mounting brackets surrounding the vehicle. The weight and bulk of slat-armor has caused rollovers, maneuverability problems, and overweight difficulties. But it does offer effective protection – the Second Stryker Brigade in Iraq sustained over 250 RPG attacks in six months with 70 direct hits, yet none penetrated.

Water cans, ration cases, barbed wire coils, airfield matting, spare track links, and sandbags have been secured to the exterior of vehicles to provide some degree of standoff. Their real value is that most hits on vehicles are at extreme angles, not even close to zero degrees impact. Such add-on enhancements greatly reduce penetration at such angles.

The most effective means of resisting RPG attacks is for vehicles to keep moving, make frequent course changes, and employ as much suppressive fire as possible. Generating smoke, by firing smoke grenades from on-board dischargers or dropping smoke grenades, is also a good preventative measure. However, this reduces the effectiveness of vehicle return fire, and creates a hazard for dismounted troops among maneuvering vehicles.

During the South African Bush War the APCs would be fired upon as soon as they halted to dismount troops. Hits on or near the vehicles could inflict casualties among the dismounts as the fragments can travel up to 150m. However, effective defensive tactics were put in place by the South African Defence Force (SADF). When taken under fire the APCs would immediately start up and turn in different directions following unprescribed circular routes. There was no specified pattern; irregularity was the key to the tactic's success, and the drivers coordinated this by radio. The circles were tightened and the APCs kept on the move, making themselves a difficult target and raising screening dust while the gunners kept up continuous suppressive fire as the RPG teams were sought out.

Watching from a distance, US Army soldiers detonate and collapse caves that could be used as weapons caches outside of Rawah, Iraq. The "slat-armor" or "birdcage armor" fitted to their Stryker M1126 infantry carrier vehicles has proved very effective as protection from RPGs, but it does increase the vehicle's weight, fuel consumption, and suspension system wear, and reduce maneuverability, and it has caused rollovers. (US Army/TSgt Andy Dunaway USAF)

73

## Bunker Tests:

**Bunker 1**

Sandbags stacked in a flat-topped pyramid    Height: 6ft (1.82m)    Width: 6ft (1.82m) bottom, 4ft (1.21m) top

**Bunker 2**

Unsupported sandbag wall with sloped front    Height: 6ft (1.82m)    Width: 12ft (3.65m)    Thickness: 4ft (1.21m) bottom, 2ft (0.61m) top

**Bunker 3**

Timber-supported sandbag wall with vertical front    Height: 8ft (2.43m)    Width:18ft (5.49m)    Thickness: 4ft (1.21m)

## Results

**Bunker 1, without standoff**    The round penetrated 60in (1.5m) into the sandbags and the tailboom continued downrange barely slowing.

**Bunker 2, with standoff**    The warhead either broke up with the tailboom penetrating 36in (1m) into the sandbags or detonating on the chain-link.

**Bunker 3, without standoff**    The round penetrated 90in (2.2m) into the sandbags after being fired into the end of the 5.49m-long wall.

**Bunker 3, with standoff**    The warhead either broke up, with the tailboom penetrating 48in (1.2m) into the sandbags, and in some instances protruding through the 2x6in (5x15cm) supporting planks, or detonating on the chain-link.

## Protecting bunkers against RPGs

In late 1967 the Combined Material Exploitation Center in Vietnam tested the RPG-2 and 7 against bunkers to determine their effects and how to protect bunkers. Three types of test bunkers were constructed of sandbags filled with packed damp, sandy laterite (gravelly) soil:

**OPPOSITE**

**1** The pyramid-shaped bunker (Bunker 1) in the RPG tests in Vietnam. This is the result of a PG-2 HEAT round impact without the chain-link fence standoff.

**2** Bunker 2, unsupported sandbag wall with chain-link and perforated steel planking (PSP) 4ft (1.21m) forward of the wall. The PSP restricted vision and return fire, was too heavy to transport, and more difficult to construct and repair.

**3** Here a PG-7 HEAT round struck the timber-supported sandbag wall (Bunker 3) without standoff protection. It penetrated 85–90in (2.16–2.29m) and it can be seen that the explosion baked the sandbag fill into hardened lumps.

**4** The results of a PG-2 round striking a timber-supported sandbag wall (Bunker 3) after detonating on the chain-link. It still penetrated 28–32in (71.1–81.3cm). Here the fencing was angled at 60 degrees in an effort to deflect the projectile, but this had no effect.

**5** A PG-7 round struck the chain-link, which shorted out the piezoelectric fuze, and the round broke up. The tailboom was still able to penetrate 36in (91.4cm) of sandbags of an unsupported sandbag wall with sloped front (Bunker 2).

**6** This PG-7 round broke up when hitting the chain-link standoff in front of a timber-supported sandbag wall (Bunker 3). The tailboom was still able to penetrate 48in (121.9cm) of sandbags and the 2x6in (5x15cm) timbers. It would not have caused any casualties, but no doubt would have been unnerving to occupants. (All images US Army)

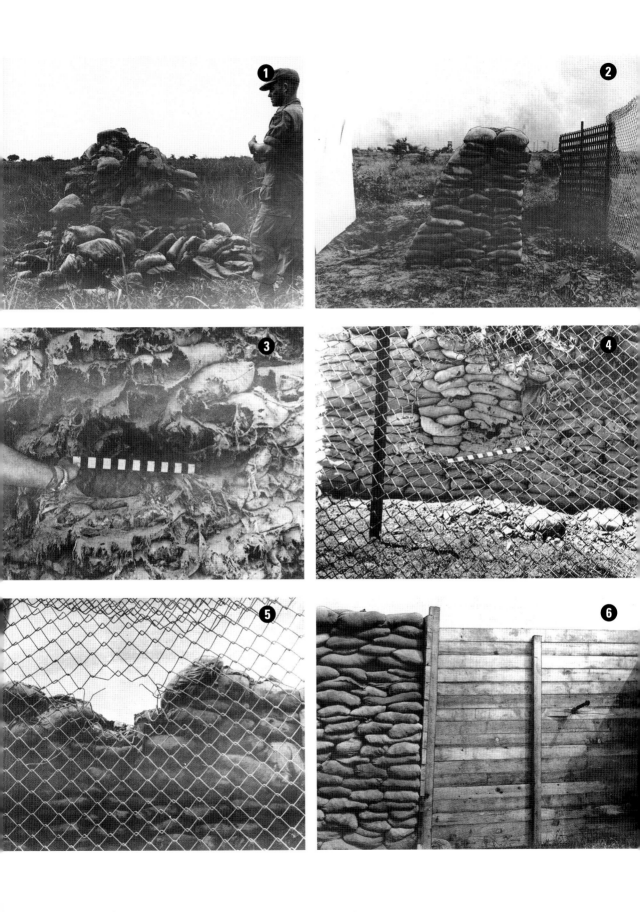

Although both the RPG-2 and 7 were used in the tests, only the RPG-7 results are provided here as RPG-2 penetration was about half that of RPG-7. The weapons were fired at a range of 50–100m using PG-7 HEAT rounds. The bunkers were fired on with and without "standoff material," that is, galvanized chain-link fencing in 57mm squares (also known as hurricane or cyclone fencing), which proved effective. Other materials tested were nylon net (which had no effect), pierced steel planking (denied visibility, very difficult to construct), and expanded steel mesh (limited visibility, difficult to construct). Masses of concertina wire were also tested and this resulted in detonations and/or broken-up projectiles. But wire and mesh were also difficult to repair while the 460–560mm hole blown in chain-link could be easily patched, so it remained the most effective option.

As a result of these tests large quantities of chain-link fencing were rushed from the United States and issued to units to erect in front of perimeter bunkers and other structures. "RPG fences" were recommended to be 6ft (2m) or 8ft (2.4m) high and erected 4–10ft (1.2–3m) in front of bunkers using 8ft (2.4m) U-shaped barbed wire pickets supported by wire anchor lines. If they were erected 20–25ft (6–7.6m) from the bunker the jet blast effect was disrupted. APCs would often carry a roll of chain-link with pickets to be erected in front of them when halting for the night. A fence 2ft (0.6m) in front of an AFV halved the round's penetration. Even at 9ft (3m) it limited the penetration to 25mm. Tests were conducted to see if chain-link erected at a 60-degree slope would help deflect the warhead, but it had the same effect as vertical chain-link.

The Rhodesians tested the effects of the RPG-7 against typical construction materials used at farm homesteads in 1979. When chain-link fencing was erected 7.6m out from 15mm and 150mm concrete walls they would not be penetrated. Double 115mm brick walls with 300mm earth or rubble fill between them was recommended for vulnerable points. The tests also found that RPGs would penetrate 2.3m of sandbags, 0.4m reinforced concrete, and 1.5m log/earth bunkers.

## Armor protection

Chain-link, bar- and slat-armor defeated RPG warheads in one of two ways. Approximately 40 percent of rounds would strike one of the wires and detonate. The fence's standoff distance from the bunker dissipated the blast to reduce its penetration into sandbags. With some 60 percent of the rounds the nose passed through the mesh opening with the light sheet metal nosecone being compressed inward to come in contact with the inner aluminum liner. This shorted out the piezoelectric contact to prevent it from detonating and caused the warhead to break up. However, the tailboom would penetrate into or even through the sandbags.

A system similar to chain-link is offered by the Swiss firm RUAG. Light Armor System against Shaped Ordnance (LASSO) consists of a very lightweight chain-link screen mounted on 300mm standoff brackets on the sides of light AFVs. However, it is prone to be torn off in dense vegetation and built-up areas.

Ceramic appliqué armor in the form of tiles glued to AFV hulls was also tested but it did little good on soft-skin vehicles. Although it was effective against heavy machine gun fire, it offered little protection from shaped-charges and added considerable weight.

In 2005 Bulgaria, with Greek and Polish participation, began development of add-on anti-RPG armor to protect helicopters and vehicles on behalf of NATO. The classified strap-on armor employs three layers of ceramics, gel, and other materials. A second belt of unspecified armor will protect a helicopter's fuel tanks and transmission from fragments generated when an RPG shatters against the armor. It is expected that up to 80 percent of rounds will be neutralized by disabling the fuze. However, it is not yet light enough to use on helicopters.

An even more advanced armor is under development. "Electric armor" consists of a highly charged capacitor connected to two separate metal plates on the AFV's exterior. The outer bulletproof plate is made from an unspecified alloy, and is grounded while the insulated inner plate is charged. It is powered off the tank's own power source, and when the tank commander is in a dangerous area he switches on the inner plate. When an RPG warhead detonates on the outer plate the jet makes contact with the inner and thousands of amps vaporize it. Testing to date has shown promise but at the time of publication it has yet to be widely adopted.

# CONCLUSION

The RPG-7 has been with us for over five decades. While new high-tech antiarmor missile systems will continue to be developed alongside simpler single-shot weapons, there is little doubt that the RPG will be with us for a long time to come. It is still being produced, along with ammunition, in at least half a dozen countries. This flexible and practical little weapon has shown so much value that it is inevitable that new types of rounds will be developed. The RPG could conceivably, perhaps in reengineered upgraded models, still be with us for another 50 years.

A major advantage of the RPG is its over-caliber projectiles. This means there are no limitations in terms of designing specialized projectiles, as there are with weapons using only full-bore projectiles – to include disposable launchers. The RPG's key advantage over single-shot launchers is that the crew can carry a variety of specialized rounds to use against a variety of different targets.

RPGs of various models, but mainly the RPG-7, are in use by at least 90 countries and by scores of guerrilla, insurgent, and terrorist organizations. They will be a continued threat not only for AFVs, but for any imaginable target. Every officer should know their capabilities and limitations, the many ways in which they have been deployed, and how to counter them. Every soldier, regardless of army, should know how to operate one. Quite simply, the RPG threat is not one that will go away.

# BIBLIOGRAPHY

Bund, Jacques F., *Warsaw Pact Weapons Handbook*, Boulder, CO: Paladin Press, 1989

Fleischer, Wolfgang, *Panzerfaust and other German Infantry Anti-tank Weapons*, Atglen, PA: Schiffer Publishing, 1994

Gander, Terry J. *The Bazooka: Hand-held Hollow-charge Anti-tank Weapons*, London: PRC Publishing, 1998

Gebhardt, James F. (translator), *The Official Soviet RPG Manual*, Boulder, CO: Paladin Press, 2006 (translation of the Soviet RPG-2 and RPG-7 manuals.)

Kopenhager, Wilfried, *Die Mot-Schützen der NVA von 1956 bis 1990*. Solingen, Germany: Barett Verlag GmbH, 1995

Kopenhager, Wilfried, *Waffen-Arsenal: Raritäten der NVA, Band 4*. Friedberg, Germany: Podzun-Pallas-Verlag GmbH, 1992

Lovi, A.A., *Otechestvennye Protivotankovye Granatomernye Kompleksy* (Russian Antitank Grenade Launcher Complexes), Moscow: Tekhnika-molodezhi; Vostochnvi Gorizont, 2001

Oliker, Olga, *Russia's Chechen Wars 1994–2000: Lessons from Urban Combat*, Santa Monica, CA: Rand Corporation, 2001

US Army, *Operator's Manual: Launcher, 40mm, RPG-7, Light Antitank Grenade (Soviet)*, Threat Analysis Center Manual ATC-T1-015-80, 1980

US Army, *Soviet RPG-7 Antitank Grenade Launcher: Capabilities and Countermeasures*, TRADOC Bulletin No. 3[u], 1976. (http://www.fas.org/man/dod-101/sys/land/row/rpg-7.pdf)

# INDEX

Figures in **bold** refer to illustrations.

Abrams, General Creighton 69
Afghanistan, fighting in 43, 47, 56, 69,
    70, 72
    weapons used 35, 41, 47, 51
AFVs, attacks on 4, 39, 42, 43, 44–5, 58, 61,
    62, 63, 64, 65, **66–7**, 72, 76, 77
airburst fragmentation projectiles **32**,
    **48–9**, 51
A-IX-1 (*geksogen*), use of 11
antiarmor rockets: AT4 71; XM132 71
antipersonnel operations 42, 51–2, 61, 64, 65
antitank grenade launchers: SPG-82 11–12
antitank grenades 6, 11, 65: RPG-43 62
antitank hand grenades 6, 7, 8, 9: RKG-3
    20, 58; RPG-6 6, 9, 21; RPG-40 6, 9;
    RPG-43 6, 9, 62
antitank missiles 58, 63: AT-3 62; Dragon
    17, 69
antitank rifle grenades 7, 8, 9: VG-45 20;
    VPGS-41 8
antitank rifles 6, 7, 11: .55in Boys 8, 12;
    PTRD-41 **8**, 9
antitank projectors 9: Mk 1 PIAT 12;
    R.Pz.B.43, 54, 54/1 13; RS-65 11;
    M1/A1/9/A9 bazooka 9, 11, 12, 13;
    *see also* RPGs
APCs, attacks on 44, 58, 59, 63, 73, 76:
    M113 59, 60, 63; M113A1 **58**, 59, 60
appliqué armor, use of 31, 44, 63, 77
Arab-Israeli wars 62, **62**: Six-Day 33; Yom
    Kippur 33, 37, 62, **62**, 69
armor, penetration of 8, 10–11, **10**, 16, 30–1,
    44, **62**

"bar-armor", use of 72, 76
barrage-fire 51, 61, 63, 64, 65, 68
"birdcage armor", use of 72, **73**
bunkers, attacks on 51, **59**, 61, 71, 74,
    **75**, 76

chain-link fencing, use of 61, 74, **75**, 76, 77
Chechen rebels 64–5, **64**, **66–7**
Chechen Wars 63, 64–5, **64**, **66–7**, 69
Chinese-built weapons/projectiles 19, **25**, **32**,
    36, **36**, 37, 38, **48–9**, 51, 59, 64, 69
CIA, and supply of RPG-7s 64

"electric armor," composition of 77
explosive reactive armor (ERA) 30–1, 42, 44,
    63, 65, **66–7**

firing positions: RPG-2 53; RPG-7 54–5
Firulin, V. K. 22
fortifications, attacks on 4, 39, 42, 47, 50, 64

German Army 7, 8, 10, 11, **12**, 13, **14**
guerrilla bands, weapons used 20, 53, 71, 78
gunner teams **17**, **28–9**, 35, 36, 53–4, 56, 58

HE/fragmentation projectiles 37, **56**, 61, 63:
    airburst **25**, **32**; OG-7 **25**, 26, **32**, 52;
    OG-7E 52; OG-7F 52; OG-7G 52;
    OG-7M 52; OG-7V **25**; OG-16 35
hearing damage 50
HEAT projectiles/warheads 6, 9, 12, **40**, 43,

44, 47, 60: PG-1 **15**, 16, 17; PG-2 11, 15,
    17, **18**, 19, **25**, **32**, 40, 74, **75**; PG-4 21,
    **21**; PG-7 11, 21, 22, **25**, 28–30, **32**, 33,
    40, 43, 74, **75**, 76; PG-7L **25**, 30; PG-7LT
    31; PG-7M 11, 22, **25**, 27, 30, 32, **32**, 40,
    68; PG-7R **25**, 30–1; PG-7S 30; PG-9 35;
    PG-16 **25**; PG-16V 35; PG-18 **34**; PG-70
    16; PG-80 17; PG-150 20, 21; TBG-7 **25**;
    Type II/III **25**
helicopters, attacks on 45–6, **46**, 47, **48–9**,
    51, 59, 64, 65, 69, 70

incendiary projectiles/rockets 39, 40, 42
Iraq, fighting in 38, **38**, 41, 42–3, **44**, 46, 47,
    53, 65, 68, 69, **56**, 70, 72, **73**
Israeli Defense Force, attacks on **62**; use of
    RPG-7 33, 62, 63

Lebanon, fighting in **61**, 63
Lomnskiy, G. P. 16

Medvedev, V. I. 30
Mohaupt, Henri J. 9
*mujahideen* (Afghanistan) 63–4, **63**, 65
Munroe, Charles E. 9

Neumann, Egon 9
night vision sights 18, 22, 26, 41, **41**, 60:
    1LH52 31, 35; 1PN58 31, **32**, 35; NSP-1
    31; NSP-2 31; NSP-3 31; PGN-1 31, 35;
    PGO-7VZ 31; Types I/II/III 37
North Korean-built weapons 19
North Vietnamese Army, tactics/weapons 19,
    **40**, 41, 46, 47, **48–9**, 59–61, **59**

optical sights 18, 36, 38, 50: AGI 3x40 39;
    RPG-1 16; RPG-2 17; RPG-7 22, **24**, 26,
    27, **28**, 35, 37, 38, 54, 55, 58, **68**; RPG-16
    35; Type 69 37

*Panssarikauhu* (Finland) 13
*Panzerfäuste* 6, 11, **12**, **13**, 14, **14**, 15: *30
    gross* 12, 13, 15; *30 klein* 12, 15; *60* 12,
    **12**, 13, **14**, 15; *100* 12, 13, 15; *150*
    12–13, 15; *250* 13, 16
*Panzerschreck* 13, 15, 16
PUS-7 sub-caliber training device 32–3

recoilless guns/rifles 6, 9, **58**, 60: M72/72A3
    LAW 29, 34, 69, 71; M136 (AT4) LAW
    71; SPG-9 34, 35, 58
Rhodesian Bush War 68, 76
Rogozin, I. E. 33
RPGs (rocket-propelled grenades) 6, 53
    defense against 59, 60, 72, 74, **75**, 76, 77
    effectiveness of 4, 42, 68, 69–70, 78
RPG-1 (LPG-44) 13, 14, 15, **15**, 16, **16**, 17
RPG-2 **6**, **16**, 17, 19, 20, 21, 40
    characteristics 18, 33
    copies of 19, **19**, 40, **40**, **48–9**, **59**
    loading and firing of **52**, 53–4
    noise signature **52**, 53, 55
    origins/production of 14, 15
    projectiles/warheads for 17, **19**, **25**
    US Army evaluation of 74, **75**, 76
    use of 4, **17**, 19, 20, 45, **52**, 53, 59, **59**, 60
RPG-2N 18, 20, 61; RPG-3 21; RPG-4 21,

21; RPG-5 21
RPG-7 (6G3) **5**, 6, 19, 20, **21**, 22
    characteristics 22, 23, 28–9, 33
    copies of 36–9, 41, **41**
    effectiveness of 33, 45, 46, 58, **66–7**, 69,
        70, 74, **75**, 76
    issuing of 62, 64
    loading and firing of 6, **23**, 29–30, **31**,
        54–6, 56, 57, 71
    projectiles/warheads for **5**, 21, 22, **24**, **25**,
        27, 28–9, **28–9**, 30, 32–3, **32**, 56, 68
    replication of 69, 70, 71–2, **71**
    US evaluation of 69, 74, **75**, 76
    use of 4, 6, **28–9**, 32–3, 38, **42–3**, **44**,
        45–6, 47, **48–9**, 50, 51, 56, 58, 59, 60–1,
        **61**, 62, **62**, 63–4, **63**, 64–5, **66–7**, 68, 69,
        70, **70**, 74, **75**, 76
RPG-7-USA 41, **41**; RPG-7D 26–7, **26**,
    34, 35, 39; RPG-7D1/2 26, 27;
    RPG-7V/V1/V2 22, 26, **32**, 38, 39;
    RPG-7W 22, **38**, 39; "RPG-8" 26;
    "RPG-9" 33; RPG-16 4, 6, **25**, **26**,
    33–4, 35, 64; "RPG-16D" 33; RPG-18
    4, 6, 34, **34**, 58, 64, 65; RPG-22 4, 6, 34,
    43, 64; RPG-26 4, 6, 34; RPG-27 4, 6,
    34; RPG-29 4, 34, 43; RPG-30 4, 6, 34;
    RPG-32 4, 34; RPG-75 4, 34; RPG-76
    4, 34; RPG-150 (RPG-400) 20–1, **21**;
    RPS-250 (RPG-7) 22

shaped-charge munitions 9–11, **10**, **18**;
    use 8, 10–11, **10**, 51
slat-armor, use of 31, 44, 72, **73**, 76
soft-skin vehicles, attacks on 4, 42, 45,
    72, 77
Somalia, fighting in 36, 47, 65, 68, 69–70, **70**
Soviet–Afghan War 53, 63–4, 65
spalling 8, 44
*Spetnaz* brigades, weapons of **26**, 35, 64
"starlight scopes" 31, **32**
strap-on armor, use of 77
Stryker combat vehicles, attacks on 72, **73**
Syrian Army 33, 62, **62**, 63

tanks, attacks on 8, 9, 44, 45, 59, 62:
    Merkava 63: Soviet Union 58, 63, 64, 65:
    T-90 65, **66–7**; United States 68: M1A1/2
    Abrams 43; M24 59; M41A3 59; M48
    60; M48A3/A5 43, 59, 60; M60A3 43;
    M551 60
thermobaric warheads 51: TBG-7 **25**, 26,
    51; GTB-7G 51; RShG-1/-2 34

US Army 44, 59, 69, 72, **73**
    evaluations: RPG-2 74, **75**, 76; RPG-7
    71, 74, **75**, 76
US Army, replication of RPG-7 70, 71–2

Viet Cong, actions/weapons of 19, 33, 46,
    47, **48–9**, 60, 61
Vietnam War 69, 70: actions in 45–6, **46**,
    47, 51, **58**, 71, 74, **75**, 76; weapons used
    6, 20, 33, 45–6, **46**, 47, **48–9**, 52, 58,
    59–61, **59**, 74, **75**, 76
Viper MILES laser simulator 71–2, **71**

Westmoreland, General James 69